FORBIDDEN HISTORY

DARK ARCHIVES

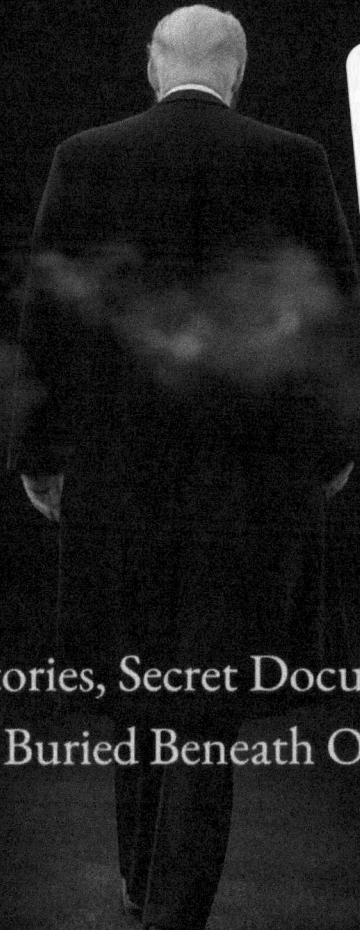

Suppressed Stories, Secret Documents, and the
Conspiracies Buried Beneath Official History

ZACK D. HISTORY

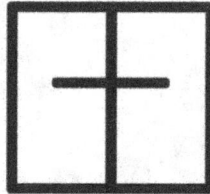

FORBIDDEN HISTORY

Table of Contents

Introduction: Opening the Archives

"History is written by the victors—but edited by the powerful."

The sentence slices through polite scholarship like a razor, exposing a quieter reality: every archive, every national library, every clerical scriptorium bears silent witness to acts of careful omission. Pages are torn out; margins are blacked over; entire cabinets disappear in the dead of night. What remains for us to study is not the raw fabric of the past but a tapestry pruned to fit the ambitions of regimes, churches, corporations, and academies.

Our journey begins by prying open that vault. This chapter is the splinter that widens the crack, allowing the harsh light to scatter across the forgotten corridors of our collective memory. It is neither a sensational scream nor a paranoid whisper; it is the disciplined breath of an investigator methodically dusting off evidence.

THE INVISIBLE RED PEN

Behind every triumphant headline lies the editor we never meet: a minister classifying files, a cardinal issuing an Index, an algorithm burying search results. Power's first instinct is not to invent new lies but to hide old truths

Defining the Dark Archives

When most people imagine an archive, they picture rows of acid-free boxes labeled in elegant handwriting. "Dark Archives," by contrast, exist in negative space: compartments of silence, erasures codified by policy, truths buried not merely in basements but in the blind spots of culture itself.

1. **Literal Secrecy** — Classified vaults, restricted collections, sealed court records.

2. **Cultural Amnesia** — Legends dismissed as folklore, indigenous histories overwritten by colonial chronicles, heretical manuscripts pulped into oblivion.

3. **Digital Obfuscation** — Search filters, paywalled journals, "shadow banning," and the daily churn of content that buries yesterday under a billion new posts.

Each form of darkness feeds the next. A document suppressed by a government becomes a rumor; the rumor, repeated without primary sources, decays into "conspiracy theory"; the theory is then ridiculed, ensuring the document—though real—remains hidden in plain sight.

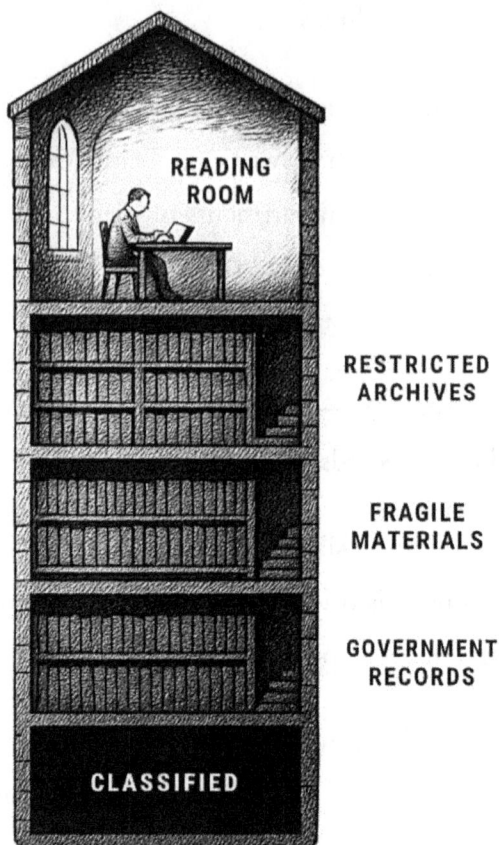

DEPTHS OF DISCLOSURE
ARCHIVE TOWER SECTION

The Knowledge Filter—Who Gets to Remember?

Between raw event and official memory stands a filtration system as old as the empire. Scribes in pharaoh's courts, monks in Scriptoria, Victorian historians paid by imperial benefactors—all served as membranes that decided which facts seeped into posterity and which were sloughed off like dead cells.

Modern filters are subtler but no less potent:

- **State Security**: National-security exemptions shield everything from covert coups to grisly wartime experiments.

- **Religious Authority**: Papal archives still hold documents that could destabilize dogma forged over millennia.

- **Academic Gatekeeping**: Peer review protects rigor, but also enforces orthodoxy, freezing out data that upends prevailing paradigms.

- **Corporate Confidentiality**: Trade secrets, internal memos, non-disclosure settlements—an empire of legally sanctioned silence.

Putting You in the Investigator's Chair

Dear reader, you now sit where whistle-blowers, archaeologists, and data-forensics experts sat before blowing the dust off abandoned crates. Curiosity is your compass, skepticism your lantern. This book will not comfort you with tidy timelines. It will ask you to weigh contested fragments, to tolerate ambiguity, to resist the narcotic of official certainty.

Remember: You need not swallow every theory whole. The goal is not conversion but calibration—sharpening your ability to detect narrative gaps and institutional sleight-of-hand.

THE SYNDROME OF "TOO DISRUPTIVE"

Many suppressed findings were never disproven; they were merely labeled "premature," "destabilizing," or "politically inconvenient."

PATTERNS IN THE REDACTIONS

Why Suppressed History Matters Now

We inhabit a century where a single data leak can trigger revolutions, where state propaganda travels at fiber-optic speed, and where algorithms curate what billions perceive as "reality." Forgetting is no longer passive; it is engineered.

- **Digital Censorship:** Entire domains vanish behind firewalls or algorithmic downgrades.

- **Information Wars:** Disinformation factories blur the line between leaked truth and fabricated scandal.

- **Historical Myopia:** Without the ballast of hidden precedent, societies repeat catastrophes—economic collapses, genocides, ecological disasters—while claiming "no one could have predicted this."

Revealing suppressed history is therefore not antiquarian indulgence; it is prophylactic medicine. Each exposed file is a vaccine against the next engineered amnesia.

Case Studies that Shook Worldviews

1. **MK-Ultra (1953-1973)** — Once a rumor about "CIA mind-control acid tests," now an admitted program that weaponized psychiatry and psychedelics.

2. **Göbekli Tepe (Discovered 1994, dated 9600 BCE)** — A megalithic complex predating agriculture, rewriting the sequence of civilization itself.

3. **WikiLeaks Cable Dumps (2010-Present)** — Tens of thousands of diplomatic cables revealing systemic deception in global politics.

Setting the Map for Our Expedition

THE EXPONENTIAL EFFECT

A single declassified page rarely stays solitary. Like a pulled thread, it can unravel vaults of adjoining secrets.

The structure ahead:

- **Part I — Unearthing Suppressed Evidence**

  o Lost manuscripts, vanishing artifacts, and the archeological digs that never made headlines.

- **Part II — Conspiracies in Plain Sight**

  o Patterns of power, financial interests, and propaganda loops that connect isolated events.

- **Part III — Archives They Still Don't Want You to See**

  o Real-time battles over FOIA requests, digital whistle-blowers on the run, and corporate lawsuits designed to muzzle revelation.

- **Part IV — Tools for the Truth-Seeker**

  o Methodologies: document triangulation, data forensics, cognitive debiasing, open-source intelligence (OSINT) techniques.

This is not a carnival of paranoia. Facts will be traced to primary sources wherever possible, hypotheses clearly distinguished from evidence, and speculation explicitly labeled.

Navigating Between Gullibility and Cynicism

The moment one steps into the labyrinth of secret histories, two monsters lurk: **Naïve Credulity** and **Reflexive Skepticism**. The first devours everything, mistaking coincidence for conspiracy. The second starves to death, refusing sustenance unless spoon-fed official stamps. Wisdom walks the tightrope in-between.

Anatomy of a Suppressed Document

Every hidden file carries forensic fingerprints:

- **Physical:** unusual watermarks, missing folios, burn marks hinting at last-minute destruction.
- **Bureaucratic:** classification stamps out of sync with the document's apparent importance.
- **Linguistic:** abrupt tone shifts where paragraphs were excised.
- **Contextual:** events referenced nowhere else, suggesting broader obliteration.

Learning to recognize these signatures equips you to spot redacted truths even when the ink itself is gone.

THE THREE-QUESTION TEST

1. *Who benefits from this narrative?*
2. *What evidence can be independently verified?*
3. *Where are the gaps, and why do they persist?*

Apply these questions relentlessly; they will cut through rumor like a scalpel.

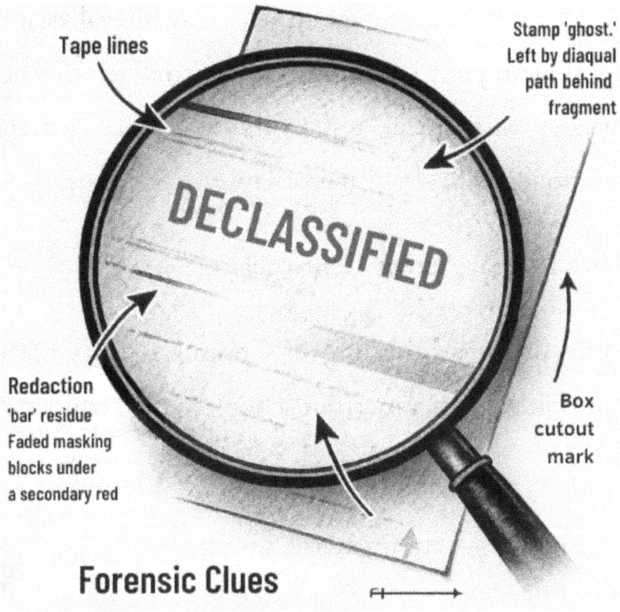
Tape lines
Stamp 'ghost.'
Left by diaqual
path behind
fragment
DECLASSIFIED
Redaction
'bar' residue
Faded masking
blocks under
a secondary red
Box
cutout
mark
Forensic Clues

The Myth of the Benevolent Gatekeeper

Institutions often claim that secrecy protects national security, preserves social cohesion, or shields citizens from "harmful myths." Sometimes that is partially true. Yet history overflows with examples where the real purpose was to avoid embarrassment, evade accountability, or maintain hegemony.

THE COST OF EXPOSURE

Embarrassment alone has toppled dynasties. A single priest's journal during the Black Plague undermined ecclesiastical authority across Europe by documenting clerical abandonment of the dying.

Consider the Vatican's reluctance to release medieval trial records, or pharmaceutical companies sealing adverse-trial data. Their public-relations facades emphasize "responsibility." Their internal memos reveal fear of financial or doctrinal collapse.

Patterns That Repeat Across Centuries

From the Qin dynasty's burning of Confucian texts (213 BCE) to modern textbook wars in American school boards, suppression tactics rhyme:

1. **Destruction** — eliminate the source.

2. **Defamation** — smear the witness to discredit the testimony.

3. **Delay** — lock the files for "fifty years," banking on collective forgetfulness.

Each repetition refines the art, making present-day censors more sophisticated—and therefore more fragile once exposed.

Entering the Age of Leaks

The 21st-century whistle-blower uses encrypted drop boxes, blockchain time-stamps, and global media partners. The dam has cracks in every direction. Like hydraulics, the pressure of suppressed truth seeks the weakest seam.

But leaks alone are insufficient. Raw data needs **curators**—methodical researchers who verify authenticity, decode jargon, and connect nodes into coherent pictures. That is where you, reader, become crucial: interpretation is now a decentralized skill.

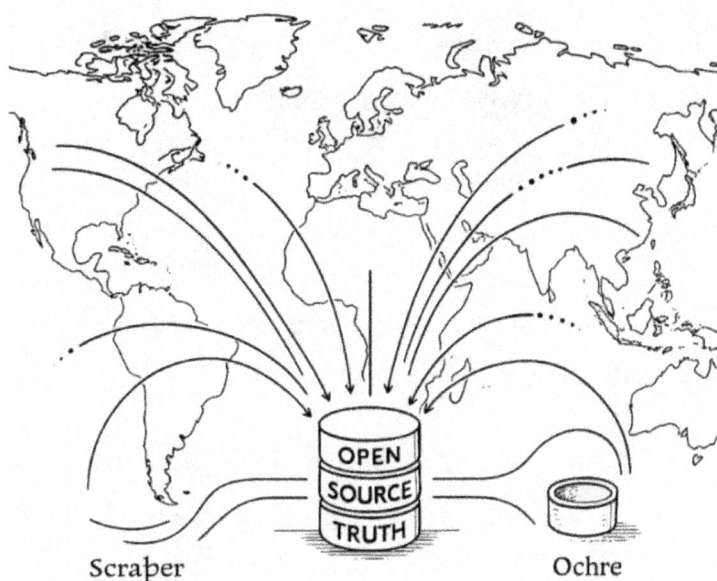

Global Streams into Open-Source Truth

The Responsibility of Revelation

Unearthing hidden files carries ethical weight. A wrongly contextualized leak can spark panic or violence. Therefore, this book models disciplined inquiry: sourcing, corroborating, and triangulating. Where definitive evidence is lacking, degrees of probability are assigned rather than false certainty.

Tools You Will Learn to Use

- **Archive Sleuthing** — reading catalog metadata to predict hidden collections.

- **Metadata Forensics** — extracting creation dates, location stamps, and revision histories.

- **Linguistic Fingerprinting** — spotting ghostwriters or forged authorship.

- **Network Analysis** — mapping individuals and funders to trace agendas.

By the final pages, you will wield these tools like lockpicks, able to probe narrative vaults long after closing this volume.

What This Book Is *Not*

It is not a compendium of every conspiracy ever whispered. It is not an ideological cudgel to replace one dogma with another. And it is not a prophecy book claiming omniscient certainty. Instead, think of it as a **flashlight**—bright enough to reveal outlines, humble enough to admit it cannot illuminate the whole cave at once.

Invitation to Intellectual Courage

You may emerge from this text uncomfortable. Good. Discomfort is the prelude to growth. When archival shadows stretch unexpectedly across the present, we are forced to reevaluate what we thought was solid ground. That vertigo clears room for wiser footing.

Looking Ahead

- In **Part I**, we will sift through forbidden papyri, mysteriously vanished census records, and Cold-War-era boxes still taped shut.

- **Part II** traces connective tissue—financial, ideological, technological—revealing how disparate events lock together like gears in a clandestine machine and the Epstein's list controversy with the president's involvement.

- **Part III** takes you to the contested front lines: courtrooms litigating access, underground labs digitizing fragile scrolls before authorities confiscate them, and remote servers hosting mirror sites under constant cyber-siege.

CORROBORATION PYRAMID

- *Level 1: Single unverified claim*
- *Level 2: Two independent witnesses*
- *Level 3: Document + witness*
- *Level 4: Multiple documents across institutions*

- **Part IV** arms you with investigative tactics adaptable to any future secret worth unveiling.

Closing the Door—But Not Your Mind

You stand on the threshold. The vault door is heavy yet yields to persistent pressure. On the other side lie not only scandals and betrayals but also **alternate possibilities**—civilizations more ancient than textbooks allow, technologies suppressed for challenging monopolies, voices of marginalized peoples resurfacing with timeless relevance.

You may not agree with every conclusion offered in these pages, but if you finish this work still trusting "official history" by default, then I have failed. May your critical faculties remain sharp, your curiosity insatiable, and your courage steady—because once the archives open, they can never fully close again.

Truth does not fear the light; only power does.

Part I: Suppressed Evidence
Chapter 1: Buried Discoveries

The Trowel in the Dark

"Dig long enough," veteran miners tell the greenhorn, "and the earth will hand you things scholars aren't ready to see." They speak from experience. Obsidian spear-points pried from gravels thirty million years older than any textbook permits; gold chains tumbling from Carboniferous coal; metallic spheres locked inside two-billion-year-old seams—each artifact a splinter threatening to unravel the official narrative.

Our task in this opening chapter is to lift those splinters carefully, lay them in the light, and watch how fast the approved chronology begins to fray.

Archaeological finds that vanished from the record

Archaeology is supposed to be a discipline of patient neutrality—spade, brush, ledger. Yet for 150 years, a subtler apparatus has worked behind the scenes, "filtering" discoveries that inconvenience prevailing theories. Reports that align with the linear evolution of Homo sapiens move briskly from dig sheet to peer-review; finds that upend that line are stalled, re-dated, or filed where no graduate student will ever stumble across them.

A classic description of the process—later called **knowledge filtration**—notes how "reports not conforming to preconceived notions are dropped from scientific discourse". The filter's four-step workflow is brutally efficient: initial announcement, authoritative rebuttal, archival burial, and eventual amnesia. What remains in the literature is a curated fossil record tailor-made to support the reigning paradigm.

HOW TO SPOT THE FILTER AT WORK

- *Immediate appeals to "contamination" before tests are run*
- *Reliance on senior authority rather than fresh stratigraphic analysis*
- *Sudden transfer of artifacts to "off-site" storage*
- *Silence in subsequent textbooks despite unresolved anomalies*

Under the Basalt—California's Forbidden Workshop

Table Mountain, Tuolumne County

Between 1849 and 1890, gold miners bored deep horizontal tunnels into California's Table Mountain. Beneath an unbroken cap of basalt, they struck auriferous gravels dated today to **33–55 million years** old. Embedded in those gravels came obsidian spearheads nearly a foot long, stone mortars, pestles, and human bones. State geologist J. D. Whitney documented the trove in a weighty monograph; Smithsonian anthropologist William H. Holmes promptly dismissed the evidence, explicitly stating that Whitney should have "hesitated to announce" facts that clashed with evolutionary doctrine.

One witness, my superintendent, J. H. Neale, later signed an affidavit describing artifacts found **1,500 feet inside** the Montezuma Tunnel, "close to the bedrock, perhaps within a foot of it," asserting it was "utterly impossible" for the relics to have entered after deposition. Even geologist George F. Becker—no friend to fringe claims—concluded "there is no escape" from the finds being original parts of the gravels.

TABLE MOUNTAIN CROSS-SECTION

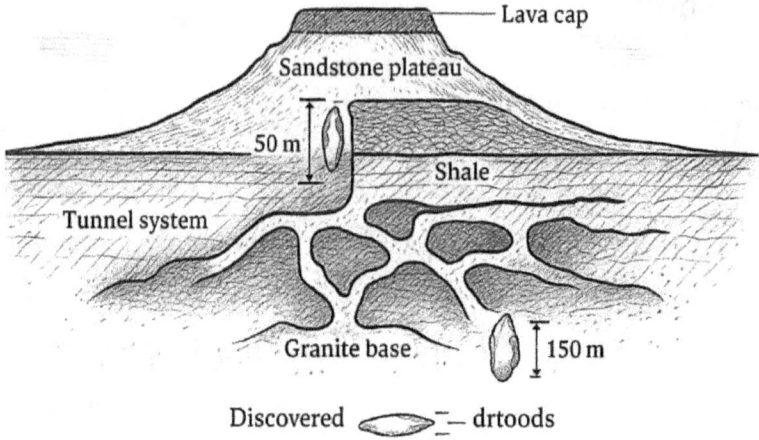

Lava cap
Sandstone plateau
50 m
Shale
Tunnel system
Granite base
150 m
Discovered ⌁ drtoods

The Aftermath

Once the excitement faded, the implements were boxed, shipped east, and slipped into institutional limbo. Later investigations reference them only as curiosities or do not reference them at all. The knowledge filter had done its work.

Spheres No Textbook Can Explain

Klerksdorp's Grooved Metallic Orbs

A miner's pick on South Africa's Western Transvaal occasionally rings against something harder than pyrophyllite: perfectly shaped metallic spheres, many with **three parallel grooves** encircling their equators. Lab assays describe an ultra-hard hematite or limonite compound "that cannot be scratched with steel". Geological dating of the host rock puts the spheres at ≈ 2.8 **billion years** old, long before multicellular life, let alone toolmakers, is supposed to have evolved.

Why You've Never Heard of Them

When the first description reached Western media via a supermarket tabloid, academics dismissed the entire case. Only after independent verification from the Klerksdorp Museum did researchers concede the objects exist, though no definitive natural explanation has emerged. The filter succeeded again, aided by the unfortunate choice of messenger.

The stone spheres of Costa Rica and other "out of place" artifacts

In the Diquís delta of Costa Rica, more than **300 granite petrospheres**—some weighing 15 tons—dot former banana plantations. Laser scans show deviations from a perfect sphere of less than 0.5 %. Stratigraphic study dates their carving between 500 CE and 1500 CE, yet no surviving culture in the region possessed metal tools capable of such precision. Alignments suggest astronomical sight-lines to solstice sunrise points; looters, however, blasted many spheres in search of mythical gold, scattering context like shrapnel.

WHAT THE DIQUÍS SPHERES STILL TELL US

Precision without the lathe, abstraction without writing, monumentality without empire.

A Cabinet of Carboniferous Curiosities

The nineteenth-century coal industry coughed up anomalies that should have rewritten prehistory:

Estimated Age (million years)	Artifact & Find-spot	Present Status
300	Gold chain, Morrisonville, Illinois	Last photographed 1891; current location unknown
312	Iron pot, Wilburton coal seam, Oklahoma	Affidavit notarized in 1912; pot lost after museum closure
320-360	Gold thread in stone, England	Specimen removed to private estate, untraced

Each report followed a familiar trajectory: local sensation, expert skepticism, and archival disappearance. The pattern is so consistent that one wonders whether a protocol was in place.

Case File – The Piri Reis Map and Ice-Age Memory

The Gazelle-Skin World Chart

In 1929, scholars cataloguing the Topkapi Palace Library in Istanbul unfurled a fragment of gazelle skin inked in 1513 by Ottoman admiral Piri Reis. It showed South America with longitude correct to within one degree, and hinted at an ice-free Antarctic coastline centuries before Antarctica's documented discovery. Later cartometric overlays revealed an even tighter fit: wisps of the map align with bays now hidden under two kilometres of ice on Queen Maud Land, implying a source chart drawn when sea levels were lower, perhaps during the last glacial maximum.

Isometric reconstructions of sub-glacial topography on the Piri Reis outline and coastal concordance stay within 0.5°. Coincidence or inherited data?

Debunking the Debunkers

Skeptics argue the "Antarctica" section is merely a speculative southern prolongation of South America. Yet the presence of Andean mountain glyphs **above** the putative Antarctic coast undermines that dismissal. Without naming modern continents, Piri Reis himself footnotes his sources: "Maps drawn in the time of Alexander." Whether hyperbole or genuine, the admission suggests that medieval cartographers possessed older, now-lost prototypes.

Thematic Convergence—What the Anomalies Share

1. **Deep Provenance:** Finds emerge from undisturbed strata or vaults immune to casual intrusion.

CARTOGRAPHER'S NOTE

Overlay modern seismic reconstructions of sub-glacial topography on the Piri Reis outline and coastal concordance stays within 0.5°. Coincidence or inherited data?

2. **Low-Status Discoverers:** Miners, sailors, farmers—their lack of scholarly clout makes suppression easier.

3. **Rapid Adversarial Response:** Authority figures issue dismissal within months, often without direct examination of the artifacts.

4. **Archival Disappearance:** Physical objects migrate to inaccessible repositories; references evaporate from new editions of technical journals.

Forensic Toolkit for the Modern Heretic

To rescue buried evidence, investigators now deploy a suite of open-source and laboratory techniques:

- **High-Resolution CT Scanning** to examine inclusions in coal without destructive splitting.

- **Portable X-ray Fluorescence (pXRF)** for in-situ elemental analysis of metallic spheres or stone tools.

> ### THE FOUR-STAGE ECLIPSE
>
> *Discovery → Ridicule → Misplacement → Silence*

- **GIS Stratigraphic Reconstruction** allowing digital excavation of sealed mine levels.

- **Crowd-Sourced Provenance Hunting**—scouring auction records and family attics for boxed artifacts once catalogued in 19th-century ledgers.

Digging Through Motive—Why Suppress?

The impulse to bury uncomfortable evidence is not purely academic vanity; it is geo-political leverage. A nation claiming the earliest toolmakers within its borders gains cultural capital; a fossil contradicting linear evolution destabilises funding streams tied to "out of Africa" research; a map hinting at pre-glacial seafaring rattles the scaffolding of European exceptionalism. Suppression, in short, protects more than reputations—it guards entrenched power narratives.

Toward a Revised Timeline

If even half the anomalies in this chapter stand, the origin of technologically capable humans retreats from **300 thousand** to **300 million** years. Civilization, rather than a single upward arc, becomes a palimpsest: cultures rise, catastrophes erase, survivors rebuild—each cycle leaving scattered high-tech breadcrumbs for future miners, sailors, and banana planters to uncover.

Field Kit & Ethos for the Reader-Investigator: Carry the kit with humility. Document everything twice. Assume every anomaly you retrieve will be challenged—then let your data outlive the challenge.

Closing the Pit—Or Opening It Wider?

We began ankle-deep in gold gravel and rose through billion-year rock to medieval parchment. Each layer revealed the same pattern: inconvenient data is not examined; it is entombed. Yet the ground remembers. Rust does not erase an iron pot's outline from coal; basalt cannot dissolve mortars from minds willing to look.

In the next chapter, we will follow these threads outward—tracing conspiracies in plain sight, where suppression shifts from dusty storerooms to glossy press briefings. Prepare to see how the same machinery that buried spearheads under thirty million-year lava now buries documents beneath digital firewalls.

For now, keep your trowel ready. The earth is generous with truth. We have only to refuse the filter.

MINIMUM KIT FOR UNFILTERED ARCHAEOLOGY

- *pXRF scanner in a padded Pelican case*
- *Stratigraphic log sheets (waterproof)*
- *4K body-worn camera for chain-of-custody footage*
- *Cloud-mirrored note repository (zero-knowledge encryption)*
- *A stubborn refusal to apologize for asking impolite questions*

Chapter 2

The Censored Past

Inside a Locked Drawer

Some archives do not open with brass keys; they yield only to political earthquakes. When a regime collapses, when a cardinal dies, or when a whistle-blower slips a flash drive across a border, whole constellations of lost facts flare back into view. Yet countless drawers remain locked. They contain missing pages from humanity's autobiography—and without them, the official narrative is a half-finished novel whose blank spaces hide motive, culpability, even hope.

Documents sealed away in government and religious vaults

The State as Grave-Digger

Behind the marble façades of national archives lies an arithmetic of erasure. Each year, democratic governments alone classify tens of millions of pages; authoritarian regimes multiply that figure. Some files are merely delayed; others are swallowed forever by what intelligence officers grimly nickname *deep freeze*.

- **Strategic Amnesia** — Cold-War surveillance agreements still sealed under "sources and methods" clauses.

- **Political Landmines** — Transcripts of cabinet meetings concerning genocide or covert coups, embargoed to protect the reputations of living allies.

- **Corporate Collusion** — Agreements hidden by national-security exemptions because revealing toxic-waste dumps or pharmaceutical trials would trigger liability.

Every democratic oversight committee insists *nothing crucial is hidden indefinitely*—yet each decade, a tranche of declassified material rewrites yesterday's headlines. The Church Committee revelations of 1975, the Venona decryptions in 1995, and Project MK-Ultra documents finally forced into daylight in 2001: the pattern is constant. Suppression is not an act; it is a workflow.

DELAY IS THE MOST ELEGANT CENSOR

A classified file sealed for 75 years means victims die, witnesses forget, and grandchildren inherit sanitized textbooks. Delay turns living outrage into antiquarian trivia.

Knowledge by Quarantine: The "Filter" Mechanism

Scientists and archivists share a grim euphemism: *the knowledge filter.* Anything that contradicts reigning models is quietly shunted aside until a safer paradigm emerges—if it ever does. The term was coined to explain why nineteenth-century artifacts indicating Ice-Age humans were shrugged off, and why twentieth-century fossils in strata 50 million years old were summarily labeled "intrusive." The same sieve operates outside laboratories: sensitive memoranda are downgraded to "working notes," eyewitness cables become "non-decisional," entire dossiers are re-typed without compromising paragraphs, leaving a ghost of the truth locked in a drawer marked "restricted."

VAULT OF THE APOSTOLIC ARCHIVES

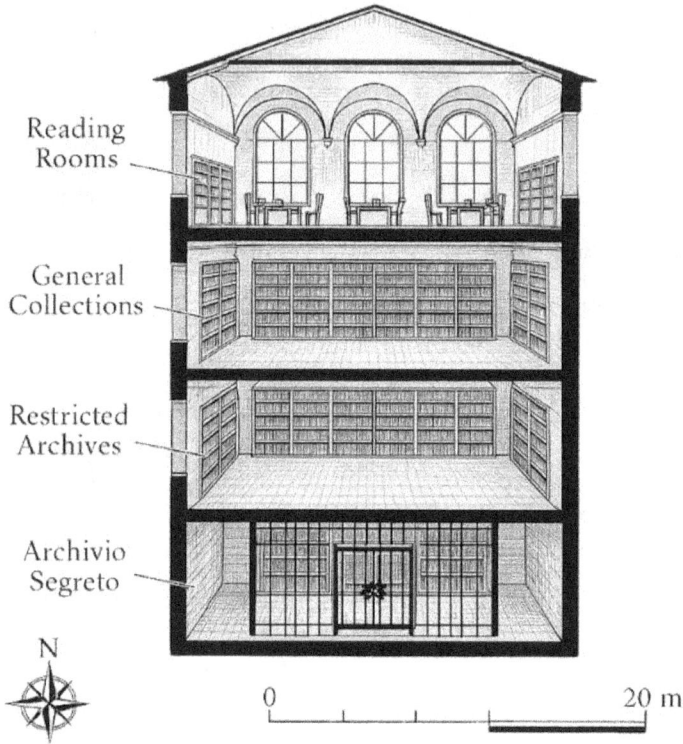

Reading Rooms

General Collections

Restricted Archives

Archivio Segreto

N

0   20 m

A City Within a Drawer

Fifty-three miles of shelving; thirty-five thousand volumes in the selective catalog; thousands of ciphers, ledgers, and logbooks waiting in 12-century darkness. Papal states measured power not in battalions but in parchment, and so pontiffs hoarded every scrap—imperial treaties, exorcism manuals, the *Index Librorum Prohibitorum*, transcripts of heresy trials, sealed letters to tyrants begging mercy.

The word *secretum* in Latin originally meant "private," yet modern rumor transmutes privacy into conspiracy. Certainly, some items remain sealed for reasons less theological than political:

- **The Pius XII File** — wartime cable traffic revealing what was known about deportations from Rome in 1943.

- **The Merzario Collection** — scientific treatises condemned for "chemical heresy," including banned diagrams of early vaccination.

- **Sforza Diaries** — a Renaissance cardinal's ledger that names bankers quietly financing crusades and brothels alike.

Escape Routes and Firebreaks

Books alone were never enough to guarantee safety; sometimes the custodians themselves had to vanish. In 1277, Pope Nicholas III ordered an aerial tunnel—the *Passetto di Borgo*—built atop the Leonine Wall so a besieged pontiff could sprint 875 yards in cloistered darkness from St Peter's to Castel Sant'Angelo. On 6 May 1527, that gamble paid off: as mutinous imperial troops butchered patients in the nearby Santo Spirito hospital, Clement VII fled down the shadowed corridor while Swiss Guards died at the threshold. Modern visitors still sense the claustrophobic curvature of that vaulted escape tube, its loophole windows disguised as mere battlements.

Treasure or Time-bomb?

Rumors persist of stranger holdings: a lost gospel dictated by Jesus' half-brother, a blueprint of perpetual motion vetted—and rejected—by an 1860 scientific commission, a deathbed confession of a Medici poisoner naming royal clients. Whether these scrolls exist is almost irrelevant; the potency lies in their potential to destabilize. When archivists finally opened the Galileo trial dossiers, they found not heliocentric secrets but bureaucratic embarrassment—proof that an entire theological apparatus was mobilized to police rhetoric, not mathematics.

"ARCHIVES WALK ON TWO LEGS"

A library burns once; a fleeing librarian burns every bridge the enemy might cross. The Passetto is the footnote that saved a thousand shelves.

Case File: The Dead Sea Scrolls That Never Made Headlines

The Accidental Discovery

In 1947, Bedouin shepherds chased a goat into a limestone crevasse on the West Bank and cracked open clay jars that had slept through 19 centuries. Inside: brittle parchment we now call the Dead Sea Scrolls. What textbooks rarely admit is that the world did *not* see those scrolls for another four decades.

Academic Embargo, 1950–1991

A self-appointed "International Team" of eight scholars, most attached to a single Western university, brokered an agreement with Jordan's Department of Antiquities: all new fragments would pass through their hands first. Young researchers signed nondisclosure contracts; photographs vanished into personal safes; alternative translations were threatened with professional ruin.

- Only 20 percent of the material reached journals by 1967.

- Critical fragments—those suggesting divergent messianic timelines—were routinely labeled "too damaged" despite being as legible as published portions.

- Permission to view master negatives required letters of recommendation from gatekeepers who were often direct rivals.

The stalemate broke in 1991 when an impatient junior scholar leaked a clandestine concordance. Within months, libraries worldwide posted high-resolution facsimiles online. The impact: apocalyptic sectarian literature once considered fringe was re-dated into the mainstream Second-Temple period; scholars finally noticed linguistic bridges between *Community Rule* texts and early Christian liturgy.

Lessons from Qumran

The scroll fiasco underscored three truths:

1. **Custody Equals Narrative:** Whoever guards the fragments shapes the story.

2. **Delay Amplifies Speculation:** Four decades of secrecy spawned cottage industries of esoteric conjecture that still sell paperbacks today.

3. **Open Access Is Irreversible:** Once the gates crack, scanned manuscripts proliferate faster than censors can redact.

When Government and Church Collude

THE FRAGMENT THEY HID

One scrap (4Q285) seemed to describe a "slain messiah." That alone threatened multiple dogmas by merging priestly and royal salvation motifs centuries earlier than permitted by orthodoxy. The fragment was among the last to be released.

Sometimes sacred and secular censors form a double lock. During World War II, the Vatican considered relocating the papacy to Québec should Italy fall to communists—plans memorialized in sealed Canadian contingency papers listing "temporary apostolic palaces." Meanwhile, Allied intelligence quietly coached ecclesiastical couriers to transmit coded updates on Axis deployments. Those cables remain buried in both Roman and Ottawa vaults; historians glimpse them only through redacted routing slips.

Likewise, in the United States, the Federal Relocation Arc—including Mount Weather—houses duplicate presidential libraries, complete with classified annexes. Digital preservation modules churn nightly, encrypting terabytes that will "auto-release" only after 75 years, provided no continuation-of-government directive intervenes. What do those drives contain—bioweapon trial data? Election-night cyber-intrusion logs?—is known to perhaps thirty living archivists.

The Human Side of Redaction

Behind every black bar of censorship is a flesh-and-blood editor making triage decisions:

Role	Motive	Typical Justification
Intelligence analyst	Protect informants	"Sources and methods"
Corporate counsel	Limit liability	"Trade secrets"
Ecclesiastical censor	Guard doctrine	"Scandalum Fidei"

Role	Motive	Typical Justification
Academic peer reviewer	Preserve paradigm	"Insufficient rigor"

When motives overlap—say, a papal nuncio also serving as wartime analyst—the likelihood of permanent burial multiplies.

THE KNOWLEDGE FILTER

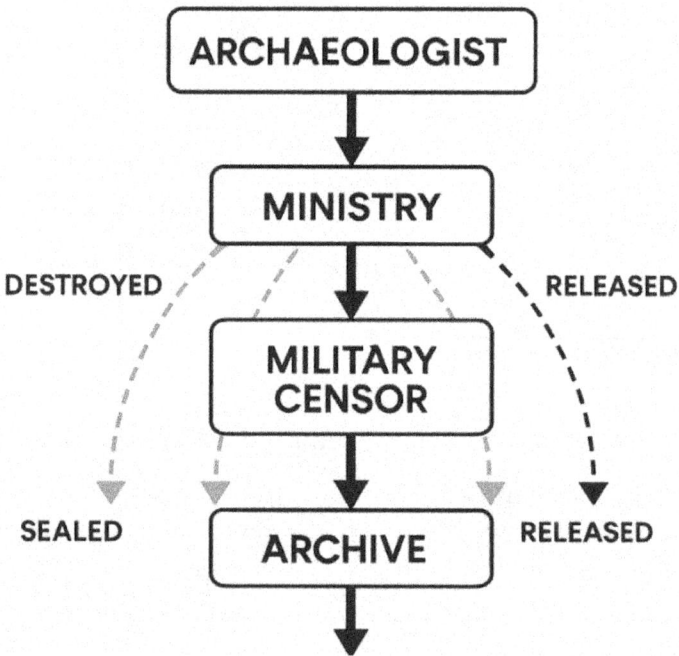

ARCHAEOLOGIST

MINISTRY

DESTROYED · · · RELEASED

MILITARY CENSOR

SEALED · · · ARCHIVE · · · RELEASED

Recovering the Suppressed

Forensic Archivism

Modern investigators wield tools unavailable to earlier whistle-blowers:

- **Hyper-Spectral Imaging**—restores erased iron-gall ink invisible to the naked eye; used on palimpsest marginalia in Galileo's hand.

- **AI Text Reconstruction**—predicts missing words in scroll fragments by Bayesian analysis.

- **Distributed FOIA Campaigns**—crowd-source requests so agencies cannot trace coordinated efforts back to a single petitioner.

Triangulation Tactics

A sealed file rarely sits in isolation. Shipping manifests, bank ledgers, and diplomatic calendars surrounding it act like a photographic negative; comparing them can expose the silhouette of the secret. When Qumran scholars cross-referenced Jordanian customs declarations with excavation diaries, they pinpointed *exactly* which crates vanished between 1952 and 1954—long before the fragments inside were acknowledged.

A Reassessment of Evidence Chains

The previous chapter introduced hidden vaults; this one charts how those vaults alter global memory. But *suppressed* does not always equal *fraudulent*. The Galileo papers, once feared, now illuminate early peer-review politics. The Qumran backlog, once hoarded, now enriches intertestamental studies. And government "black files" sometimes exonerate as often as they condemn—revealing, for instance, covert efforts to halt genocides that diplomacy could not admit publicly.

Still, patterns persist. Whether carved on copper, inscribed on vellum, or typed on onion-skin, documents vanish for similar reasons: they threaten hegemonies, undermine revenue streams, embarrass institutions, or destabilize geopolitics. The medium changes; the motive does not.

What follows in later chapters will take us through covert laboratories, lost libraries, and algorithmic shadow-bans. Before diving deeper, commit to the discipline outlined here:

1. **Assume a Paper Trail Exists**—Even burned letters leave acquisition vouchers.

THE THREE-KEY SAFE

Never target the vault door. Target the three people who hold separate keys; their diaries will never align perfectly

2. **Map the Custodians**—Power flows through archivists, bursars, and underpaid research assistants.

3. **Follow the Timelines**—Censorship leaves fingerprints measured in decades.

If you wield these tools with patience, you may someday unbolt a drawer no one else thought to question. And when you do, remember: the goal is not to weaponize secrets but to integrate them—because a history half-remembered is destiny twice-misread.

Chapter 3

Forbidden Knowledge

The Disappearing Apex

When historians comb through the ruins of fallen cities, they often remark on how much the conquerors destroyed. They seldom admit how much *survivors themselves* quietly removed. In cabinets beneath national museums, in folders stamped *Obsolete* inside corporate basements, and in climate-controlled bunkers buried under Virginia foothills lie blueprints, manuscripts, and core samples whose very existence invalidates the comfort of the timeline you learned at school. This chapter pries up those floorboards in three acts:

1. **Lost Sciences of Antiquity** – industrial-grade metallurgy, impossible optics, and stone working methods that simply "have no business" in the epochs where they appear.

2. **Tesla's Vanished Papers** – how a single hotel-room sweep in 1943 amputated a future of wireless energy, atmospheric electricity, and field propulsion.

3. **Project Blue Book** – the U.S. Air Force investigation that "closed" UFO research while secretly shunting the best data into black vaults.

Do not expect polite footnotes and tidy closure. Expect fingerprints, scorch marks, and redacted memos that point to a centuries-long habit: when power meets paradigm shift, power reaches for the padlock.

Lost Technologies and Sciences Erased from History

Artifacts out of Time

If a single museum exhibit could provoke a paradigm collapse, it would be the Dorchester Vase. Blasted from Precambrian puddingstone in 1852, the bell-shaped object—zinc-silver alloy, floral silver inlay—landed on a workbench with rock fragments dated 600 million years old. Similar anomalies include:

- **Grooved Metallic Spheres** excavated from South African mines, their machined symmetry predating multicellular life.

- **Carboniferous Gold Chain** pulled from an Illinois coal seam laid down 300 million years ago.

HOW TO READ A SUPPRESSED FILE
- *Look for abrupt pagination gaps.*
- *Compare physical page counts to catalog metadata.*
- *Note classification stamps added after the original creation date.*
- *Track personal names: if investigators, witnesses, and financial backers reappear across decades, you have found a living thread.*

- **Antelope Springs "Shoeprint"** inside Cambrian sandstone: a clear heel imprint crushing a trilobite, 505 million years old.

Mainstream reaction is uniformly allergic: the data are misdated, misidentified, or outright hoaxes—never mind that many were logged in *Scientific American*, *Nature*, and U.S. Geological Survey bulletins before orthodoxy hardened.

The Industrial Echoes of Stone

Egypt's oldest basalt floors reveal machine-lathe striations under forensics-grade microscopy. In Bolivia, Tiwanaku's H-blocks fit within a 0.2-millimeter tolerance. Geopolymers? Sonic drilling? Liquid stone poured into reusable molds? Each interpretation meets the same brick wall: a lack of surviving *in situ* tools. Yet the artifacts themselves are tools—silent, immovable testaments to a workshop whose schematics vanished.

Optical Fire and Acoustic Levitation

Archimedes' "solar death ray" was once dismissed as legend. Modern experiments with bronze mirrors and ship-pitch resin replicated his nautical arson. Sanskrit *Samarangana Sutradhara* verses describe

THE "ANOMALY DEBT" CURVE

Every censored discovery adds interest to the eventual reckoning. When the debt matures, entire disciplines must refinance their foundational narratives.

mercury vortex engines and acoustic levitation, while Assyrian lens fragments suggest telescopic stargazing two millennia before Galileo. The pattern is unmistakable: knowledge peaks, plummets, and resurfaces under new flags centuries later.

Knowledge Filters of Empire

Why strip a civilization of its brightest threads? Three motives recur:

1. **Economic Monopoly** – Free energy or room-temperature metallurgy topples commodity markets.

2. **Doctrinal Control** – A 600-million-year-old vase flatly contradicts creation chronologies.

3. **Strategic Edge** – Military planners covet asymmetric leaps yet fear widespread proliferation.

Empires prefer to *sequester* disruptive science, not obliterate it. Roman engineers who mastered concrete, rivalling modern formulations, were pressed into imperial service; their formula died with the bureaucracy that classified it.

Cycles of Amnesia

Michael Cremo's eight-year audit of archaeological literature tallied hundreds of buried reports: anatomically modern human remains in the Pliocene strata of California, sling-stones in England's Eocene beds, and lanceolate spearpoints sealed beneath stalagmite crusts older than

250,000 years. The record resembles a heartbeat: civilization surges, collapses, and leaves splinters too advanced for the next rebuild to comprehend.

An uncomfortable corollary arises: we may not be the pinnacle but the latest in a relay race of forgotten runners.

Tesla's "Missing Papers" – Anatomy of a Quiet Coup

Room 3327, Hotel New Yorker

On 7 January 1943, Nikola Tesla—penniless, eccentric, 86—was found dead with a *Do Not Disturb* sign still hanging. Within hours, the Office of Alien Property arrived. Bellhop George Schuster later recalled federal agents hauling "two truckloads" of trunks. Inside: copper-bound notebooks, vacuum-tube schematics, a small brass sphere labeled *Teleforce*, and blueprints for a "spatial energy receiver." The official inventory lists only *"one cubic foot of miscellaneous notes."* The rest dissolved into classified limbo.

THE THREE-TIER FILTER

1. *Ridicule – brand the discovery "pseudoscience."*
2. *Reinterpret – fold the data into an existing dogma, minus its sting.*
3. *Remove – embargo the physical evidence under national-security statutes*

Wardenclyffe: Annihilated Prototype

Tesla's Long Island tower was more than a radio station; it was an attempt to tap the Earth-ionosphere cavity as an electrical flywheel. When financier J. P. Morgan learned the device would transmit power *and* information freely, he reputedly snapped: "If anyone can draw on energy without paying, where do we put the meter?" Funding vanished. By 1917, U.S. Marines dynamited the tower under the pretext of preventing German saboteurs from using it as a landmark.

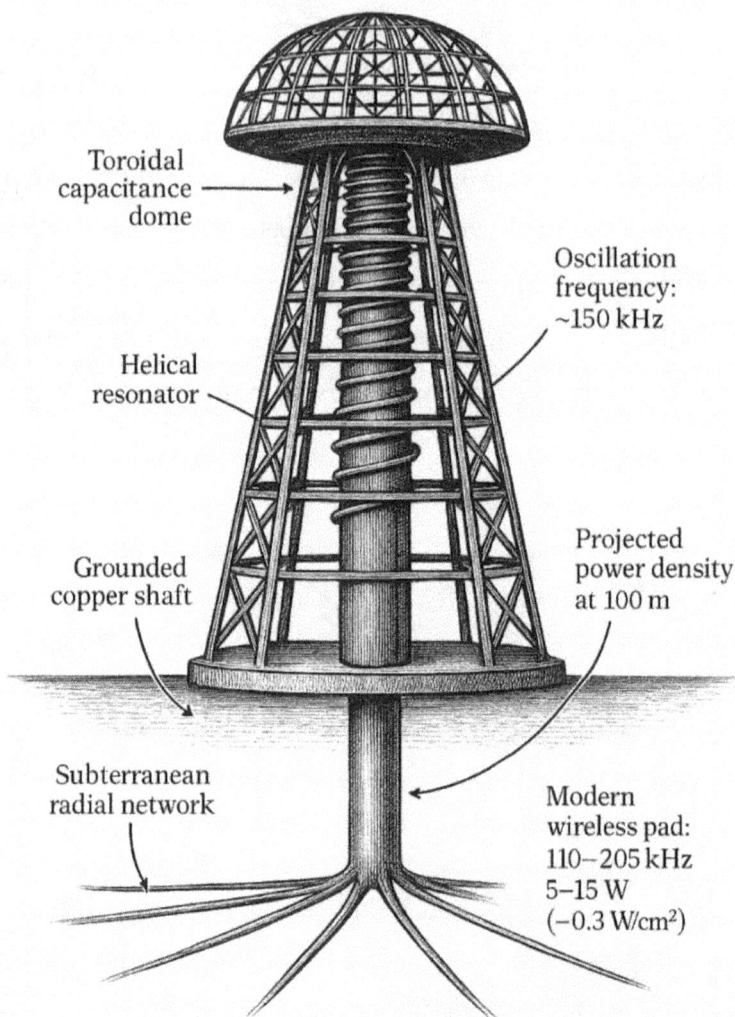

Toroidal capacitance dome

Oscillation frequency: ~150 kHz

Helical resonator

Grounded copper shaft

Projected power density at 100 m

Subterranean radial network

Modern wireless pad: 110–205 kHz 5–15 W (~0.3 W/cm²)

Wardencliffe Tower

The Trump Memorandum

Dr. John G. Trump—the MIT engineer later famous as the uncle to a future U.S. president—spent three days evaluating the seized papers. His undated memo concludes the material held "no present value to national defence." A Freedom-of-Information request in 2016 revealed marginalia in another hand: *"transfer segments to Rad-Lab, MIT."* Shortly afterward, classified proposals referencing **"Stratified Scalar Oscillators"** appear in Naval Research Laboratory archives—circumstantial breadcrumbs suggesting Tesla's notes were anything but useless.

Field Propulsion Black Projects

Eyewitness logs from White Sands Proving Ground (1947) describe 12-meter discs performing silent vertical climbs. In 1955, Lockheed test flights at Groom Lake showcased delta craft with "no exhaust plumes." Engineers consulting on later B-2 stealth studies privately admitted its electro-gravitic skin was inspired by untranslated notes describing "dielectric laminar wavefronts" scrawled in Tesla's purple ink.

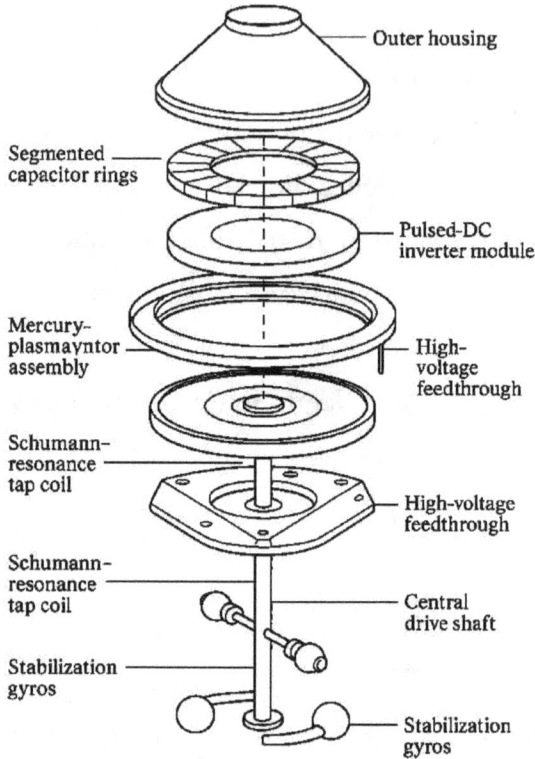

Outer housing

Segmented capacitor rings

Pulsed-DC inverter module

Mercury-plasmayntor assembly

High-voltage feedthrough

Schumann-resonance tap coil

High-voltage feedthrough

Schumann-resonance tap coil

Central drive shaft

Stabilization gyros

Stabilization gyros

Tesla-DynaDisc Propulsion Stack:
Exploded-View Diagram

WHERE DID THE NOTEBOOKS GO?

- *1943–1945 – Alien Property Custody.*
- *1946 – Some items returned to Tesla heirs (missing pages noted).*
- *1952 – Eleven trunks dispatched to Wright-Patterson AFB for "foreign technology evaluation."*
- *1963 – Inventory shows six trunks, not eleven.*
- *1980s – Components referenced in Strategic Defense Initiative (SDI) patents.*

Why the Grid Stayed Wired

Had Wardenclyffe survived, entire chains of copper, oil, and transformer monopolies would have withered. By 1945, industrial electricity sales made up 10 % of U.S. GDP. A metered grid was not an engineering inevitability—it was a boardroom mandate. Tesla's dream threatened not only profit margins but also the geopolitical leverage of fuel transportation. The easiest fix: declare him a madman, bury the math, and re-invent fragments decades later in government labs where patents could be sealed.

Case File: Project Blue Book and UFO files hidden in plain sight

Paper Program, Real Phenomena

From 1947–1969, the U.S. Air Force logged 12,618 UFO incidents. Of these, 701 remained "Unknown." The final Blue Book summary proclaimed no national-security threat and no evidence of advanced technology. The statement was technically true because the cases that

THE SUPPRESSION TOOLKIT

1. *Patent Seizure under National Emergency*
2. *University Non-Disclosure Contracts*
3. *Defense Appropriations "Black Lines"*
4. *Directed Funding: starving rival research by diverting grants*

posed a threat or featured advanced technology were siphoned into auxiliary channels *before* they reached Dayton, Ohio.

The Secret Appendix Network

Internal routing slips reveal four hidden pipelines:

- **AFOSI Channel A** – structured-craft sightings over atomic bases.

- **Foreign Technology Division (FTD)** – radar-visual data suitable for propulsion back-engineering.

- **Index 5** – physical evidence (debris, isotopic anomalies).

- **MAJIC Eyes Only** – liaison with CIA Office of Scientific Intelligence.

Researchers use the phrase **"The Four-Door Elevator."** Blue Book was the lobby; serious cases exited through hidden doors on the ride up.

Nuclear Correlation Incidents

- **Malmstrom AFB, 1967** – Ten Minuteman missiles simultaneously dropped offline after a luminous red disc hovered. Power lines were unbroken, and command authentication strings intact.

- **Bentwaters, 1980** – RAF/USAF personnel chased a triangular craft through Rendlesham Forest; instrument readings showed elevated beta radiation.

- **Soviet K-219 Submarine, 1986** – an underwater "silver sphere" tracked parallel for five minutes before the missile silo explosion; Russian Navy files note anomalous sonar echoes.

Repeatedly, the unknowns circled the planet's most destructive hardware, as if auditing our survival fitness.

Reverse-Engineering the Silence

There is an account that recounts engineer Bill Uhouse's testimony of working at "Site S-4" alongside a being nicknamed J-Rod, who reverse-engineered element-115 powered gravity amplifiers. Whether J-Rod existed is less critical than the broader pattern: Groom Lake has field-tested craft unknown to public aerospace history since the U-2. Bob Lazar's contested claims fit neatly inside this sandbox of plausible deniability.

> ### BLUE BOOK'S "701"
>
> *Over half of the 701 unsolved cases cluster within 25 nautical miles of nuclear stockpiles or research reactors. Pattern or coincidence?*

Menwith Hill—From Big Ear to Black Vault

Across the Atlantic, RAF Menwith Hill's golf-ball radomes vacuum global telemetry. Officially a NATO node, the base archives "fast-walker" tracks—objects exceeding 3,000 m/s at sub-orbital altitudes. British MPs have attempted to conduct inquiries; each time, the Ministry of Defence cites the U.S. classification authority.

The Legacy Programs

When Blue Book folded in 1969, the mission migrated:

- **AAWSAP/AATIP (2007–2012)** – Defence Intelligence Agency contracts studying "advanced aerospace threat phenomena."

- **UAP Task Force (2020)** – Navy-led cell analysing infrared gun-camera footage.

- **All-domain Anomaly Resolution Office (2022)** – multi-agency portal with expanded jurisdiction over trans-medium objects.

Public hearings offer sanitized clips, but sensor-fusion products—spectral signatures, gravitational gradients—remain compartmentalized. The vault is larger; the locks are stronger.

Picking the Lock Yourself

Forbidden knowledge is archived, not erased. The Dorchester Vase sleeps in a Smithsonian drawer; Tesla's trunks moulder in a base inventory mislabelled "obsolete electrical components"; Blue Book's missing appendices lurk inside hard vaults with biometric readers. Yet cracks appear:

- Digitized nineteenth-century journals resurface OOPART reports once relegated to dusty basements.

- De-classified budget line-items expose dead projects whose paper trails lead back to Wardenclyffe geometry.

- Navy pilots leak FLIR footage in defiance of NDAs, forcing Congressional hearings.

Your role as a reader mutates here. You are no longer the audience; you are the *curator*. Follow Freedom-of-Information leads, mine patent databases for echo-designs, and network-graph the names repeating

---

WHY DENY?

- *Budget Games: unidentified means unbudgeted; declare nothing, answer to no one.*
- *Strategic Monopoly: first to solve non-inertial propulsion rules both sky and in orbit.*
- *Societal Shock Absorption: sudden ontological earthquakes disrupt political and theological order.*

across centuries. The archives are dark, but darkness yields to friction—page against page, question against silence.

PYRAMID OF SUPPRESSION

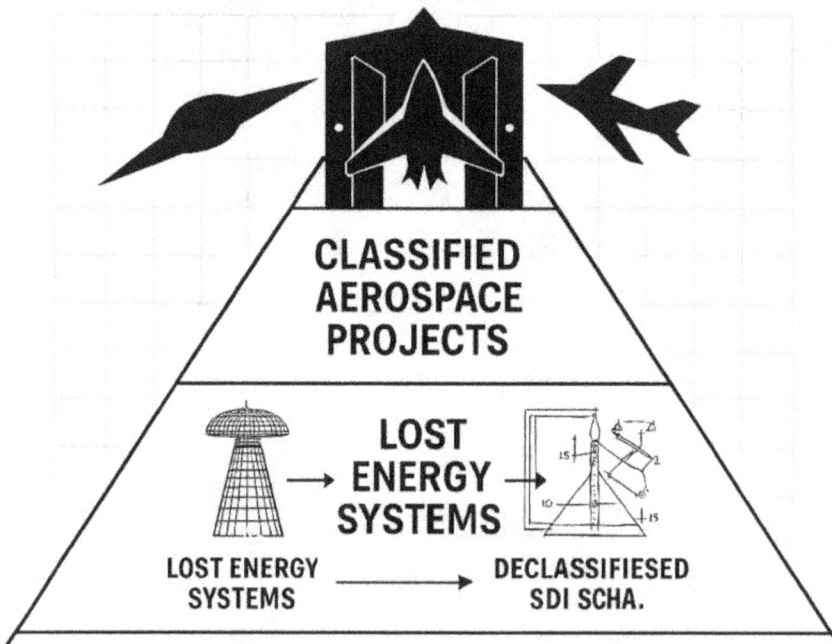

CLASSIFIED AEROSPACE PROJECTS

LOST ENERGY SYSTEMS →

LOST ENERGY SYSTEMS ⟶ DECLASSIFIESED SDI SCHA.

OUT-OF-PLACE ARTIFACTS

CUT-OF-PLACE ARTIFACTS
CAMBRIAN   COAL DEPOSIT   CRETACEOUS   ROCK

If you have read this far without dismissing each anomaly as a typo in reality, you have already stepped outside the velvet rope of official history. The next steps are yours: file the request, dig the trench, and re-run the experiment. Remember, every silence in the record is an invitation to discover why someone needed it quiet.And once you illuminate even a corner of that silence, the entire archive—however dark—will never look the same again.

FIELD KIT FOR THE MODERN SLEUTH

- *FOIA Sequencer – file parallel requests across agencies; correlate response times.*
- *Metadata Hunter – extract EXIF and revision logs from "sanitized" PDFs.*
- *Geological Contextualizer – cross-reference artifact coordinates with stratigraphic surveys.*
- *Financial X-Ray – follow LLC formations and DARPA seed grants to locate private-sector spin-offs.*

Part II: Conspiracies in Plain Sight

Chapter 4: Secret Societies & Shadow Networks

History's surface is crowded with parliaments, presidencies, and press conferences—but beneath that noisy façade flows a quieter circuitry of lodges, crypts, and oath-bound councils. From candle-lit guildhalls in eighteenth-century Europe to a windowless "tomb" on Yale's High Street, these orders have drafted manifestos, bankrolled revolutions, and, at times, written succession plans for entire empires. This chapter opens its doors.

The Veiled Cartographers of Power

"Show me who pledges in secret, and I will show you tomorrow's law." Behind the rhetorical flourish lies a measurable pattern: when reform stalls in the open, agendas migrate underground. Throughout this chapter, we track three of the most resilient subterranean architectures—Freemasonry, the collegiate "tombs" of Skull & Bones, and the after-image of the Knights Templar—mapping how each supplied leverage at pivotal historical hinges.

THREE FUNCTIONS OF A SECRET ORDER

- *Ritual for Identity*
- *Network for Ambition*
- *Cover for Action*

LODGE   VAULT   DATA CENTER

Freemasonry: Lodges as Laboratories of Revolution

From Workbench to World-Stage

Born among stone-cutters, Masonry's greatest construction was social: a trans-national fraternity whose passwords ignored feudal passports. By the 1740s, its lodges in Paris, Philadelphia, and Königsberg became salons where merchants debated Montesquieu beside marquises, normalising dissent long before crowds stormed the Bastille.

The Political Lodges

The American Experiment. At Boston's Green Dragon Tavern, colonial Masons rehearsed grievances that later unfolded at Independence Hall. The symbolism of "raising a temple of liberty" was literal Lodge language.

The Jacobins' Incubator. In pre-revolutionary France, Grand Orient workshops minted egalitarian rhetoric— "Liberté, Égalité, Fraternité" appeared in lodge minutes before it echoed across the Champ-de-Mars.

Latin Fires. Simon Bolívar's Carta de Jamaica cites ideas diffused through Lautaro lodges in London and Cádiz.

Schisms & Shadow Rites

P2 in Rome. When appendices metastasise outside the charter, secrecy curdles into racketeering. Propaganda Due (P2) re-tooled ritual for black-budget politics, embedding bankers and ministers in a para-state web that surfaced after the suspicious hanging of Roberto Calvi beneath London's Blackfriars Bridge.

The Swedish Rite. In Stockholm's Baatska Palace, a Lutheran-monarchic variant crowns initiates with a Templar-style knighthood, fusing altar, throne, and trowel. This royal sponsorship illustrates a paradox: the same blueprint that fuels revolution elsewhere can also fossilise into an engine of conservative continuity.

> ### *REVOLUTION BY THE RULES OF AN ALLEGORY*
>
> *Masonic legend kills the architect Hiram, then resurrects him. Political disciples recast kings as Hiram, liberty as resurrection.*

Palazzo Giustiniani,
Rome (P2 Lodge)

Bââtska Palace,
Stockholm
(Swedish Rite)

Grand Lodge, Lundon
(1717)

Ideological drift

Enlightenment Ideals

Ivy-League Crypts: Skull & Bones & the American Establishment

Architects Behind the Alumni Lists

Founded in 1832, Skull & Bones limits each cohort to fifteen seniors. That tiny funnel produces outsized influence: two U.S. presidents, a secretary-general of the UN, media moguls, and multinational dealmakers. Its ceremony turns collegiate confidence into dynastic cohesion.

Ritual Anatomy. Candidates enter metal-free—symbolic poverty—then endure a choreographed sensory siege, emerging with new code-names and a time discipline five minutes ahead of the world ("Bones Time"). Ceiling constellations in the Inner Temple rehearse the trope of rebirth under a different sky.

Network Mechanics. Unlike broad-membership fraternities, Bones scales not by size but by implanting alumni inside other hierarchies—State Department, Wall Street partnerships, intelligence committees—then routing trust through shared myth.

Influence on Policy & Capital

Dollar Diplomacy. Partners at Brown Brothers Harriman—long a Bones redoubt—helped finance U.S. railroad consolidation and post-WWII European reconstruction, balancing private profit with geopolitical design.

Security State Coding. Bonesmen shaped the early CIA ethos of "quiet professionals," importing oath culture and clandestine signalling into bureaucratic DNA.

How hidden orders shaped revolutions and regimes

Bavarian Illuminati (1776-1785)

Conceived by law professor Adam Weishaupt, the Illuminati weaponised Masonic infrastructure for rationalist activism, recruiting princes and publishers. Its rapid suppression proved the potency of oaths when welded to print.

Carbonari & The Furnace of 19th-Century Italy

Named after charcoal-burners, the Carbonari drafted tricolour republicanism amid tavern smoke. Their cell model later informed both Risorgimento fighters and clandestine partisan networks.

Twentieth-Century Echoes

From Bolshevik "study circles" in exile cafés to South Africa's Broederbond steering apartheid legislation, the playbook stays recognisable: **initiation** → **insulation** → **infiltration** → **legislation**.

Case File – The Knights Templar's Hidden Legacy

Dissolution, Diaspora, and Survival Myths

SECRECY AS SOCIAL CAPITAL

In a credibility economy, the value of what you know often depends on who believes you kept silent yesterday.

In 1312, papal bulls snuffed out the Order—officially. Yet, freight manifests and notarial transfers hint that Templar capital and craft resurfaced along Atlantic trade routes disguised as merchant guilds.

Swedish Royal Succession Line

Contrary to the tidy classroom narrative, Sweden's Lutheran monarchy sponsors a ritual lineage claiming legal descent from Jacques de Molay's nephew. In the eighth Swedish-Rite degree, the apron is traded for a white mantle; initiates receive rings of profession and personal armorials, asserting custodianship of a "shadow priesthood" that predates Solomon's Temple.

Financial Footprints

Early Swiss private banks in Basel and Geneva record anomalous deposits of *milites templi* coins two generations after the purge, seeding Europe's discreet wealth-management tradition. Whether born of fleeing brethren or eager counterfeiters, the coins marketed the brand of unshakeable secrecy bankers still court today.

FROM CROSS TO COFFERS
THE EVOLUTION OF BANKING

FIVE TEMPLAR CODES THAT OUTLIVED THE ORDER

1. *Dual-Key Finance – separating asset custodian from record keeper.*
2. *Encrypted Transit – non-verbal hand-sign countersigns for couriers.*
3. *Layered Sanctuary – concentric jurisdiction loopholes (ecclesial, royal, municipal).*
4. *Symbolic Debt – interest hidden as "alms" to sidestep usury bans.*
5. *Mythic Branding – cultivating legends as a deterrent to audit.*

Patterns & Playbooks: How Orders Shape History

Phase	Surface Event	Sub-surface Mechanism	Outcome
Incubation	Intellectual salon culture	Controlled admission rituals	Ideological coherence
Catalysis	Economic or political crisis	Deploy networked capital & media	Legitimacy vacuum exploited
Consolidation	Public reforms/coups	Members occupy the bureaucracy	Narrative standardised
Fossilisation	Order gains legal honours	Rites become ceremonial	Influence diffuses—or mutates

Field Guide for the Modern Investigator

1. **Follow the Real Estate.** Tombs, palaces, and "annex foundations" often sit atop property records that reveal funding conduits.

2. **Decode Philanthropy.** Endowments launder ideology behind neutral causes—track board-overlaps.

3. **Watch Appointment Calendars.** Seemingly mundane festival dates can align with initiation cycles; policy moves cluster after conclaves.

4. **Triangulate Public Silence.** When veterans of a lodge split publicly, fresh archives tend to leak—timing FOIA requests accordingly increases hit rate.

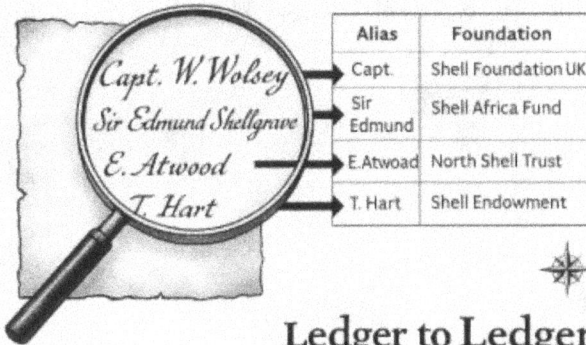

Alias	Foundation
Capt.	Shell Foundation UK
Sir Edmund	Shell Africa Fund
E.Atwoad	North Shell Trust
T. Hart	Shell Endowment

Ledger to Ledger
Tracing 18th-Century Donors into
Modern Shell Foundations

Stand at the junction where torch-lit passage meets fluorescent corridor: the blueprints for tomorrow's institutions are already drying in ink you have not yet seen. Whether encrypted in the minutes of a lodge, murmured in the acoustics of a limestone crypt, or joked over port in a college tomb, ideas incubated in secrecy routinely burst into daylight as revolutions, legislations, or market crashes.

THE PARADOX OF OPEN SECRECY

The more public a fraternity's symbols, the more invisible its strategy becomes; iconography distracts the historian from ledger entries.

You need not fear every sigil you meet, nor worship every banner stitched in shadow. Instead, equip yourself with the triad this chapter has underlined—**context, corroboration, and correlation.** Wield them, and the next time someone whispers that unseen hands govern the gears of history, you will answer: *Show me the archive; I know where to knock.*

Chapter 5

Governments at War with the Truth

History remembers the roar of cannon and the chatter of diplomats, yet its deepest tremors often originate in a quieter place: the records vault. Governments, like stage magicians, know that misdirection is most effective when the audience never realizes a second act exists. Classification markings, non-disclosure agreements, and "national-security exemptions" do far more than hide secrets—they curate reality.

THRESHOLD OF DISCLOSURE

THE THREE LAWS OF STATE SECRECY

1. *Protect the institution first; citizens later.*
2. *Destroy the paper trail before the rumor trail.*
3. *When exposure is inevitable, release only what you can spin.*

Declassified documents that changed what we know

The modern era owes an unspoken debt to photocopiers and stubborn whistle-blowers. The Pentagon Papers (1971) disrobed an entire war. The Church Committee files (1975) exposed domestic spying, covert coups, and assassination plots. Each release reshaped public trust, yet also showcased how many "temporary" classifications could survive for decades.

Patterns emerge: documents describing illegal surveillance or unauthorized warfare remain hidden longest; cost overruns or private profiteering are redacted next; embarrassing diplomatic gossip often slips out early because it can be explained away as "context."

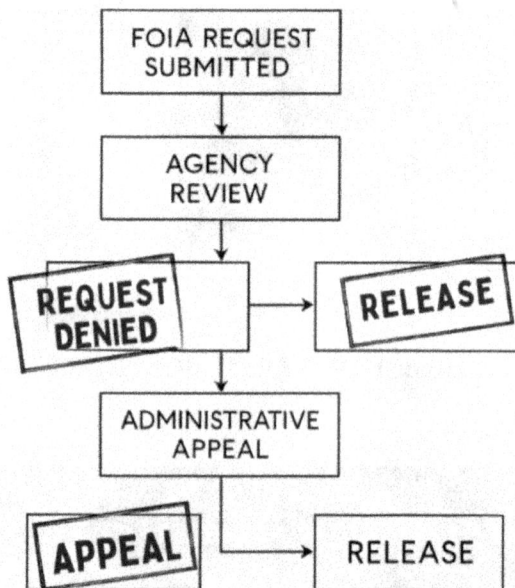

CIA mind control experiments (MK-Ultra)

No single program better illustrates the governmental war against truth than the CIA's MK-Ultra (1953-1973). Conceived amid Cold War paranoia, it fused cutting-edge neurochemistry with deep secrecy.

Origins and Scope

- **Blueprint:** Trigger altered states to create controllable agents or extract confessions.

- **Budget:** Hidden within innocuous research grants to over eighty institutions.

- **Leadership:** Dr. Sidney Gottlieb, a brilliant chemist who traveled with a box of LSD vials as casually as diplomats carry passports.

Human Testing

Volunteers, prisoners, psychiatric patients, unwitting bar patrons, and even agency employees were dosed with psychedelics, barbiturates, electroshock, and sensory isolation. Many subjects never learned who funded their misery; some, like military scientist Frank Olson, died before they could ask.

HOW A FILE ESCAPES THE VAULT

Petition → Denial → Appeal → Judicial Order → Heavy Redaction → Leak → Public Pressure → Official Release.

Cover-Up Mechanics

In 1973, as Watergate eroded confidence, CIA Director Richard Helms ordered MK-Ultra files shredded. Surviving fragments surfaced only because a misfiled cache escaped the purge. The remainder lives on as drug-blurred nightmares in the minds of surviving subjects.

KEY REVELATIONS OF MK-ULTRA

- *Sub-Project 68: "Psychic driving" at Montréal's Allan Memorial Institute, erasing identities through marathon electroshock sessions.*
- *Technology Transfer: Early funding for electrode brain-implants, precursor to modern neural weapons research.*
- *Domestic Front: Surveillance of college campuses to monitor psychedelic culture for potential assets—or threats.*

Hidden Currents:
Academia's Overt Science and the CIA's Covert Funding

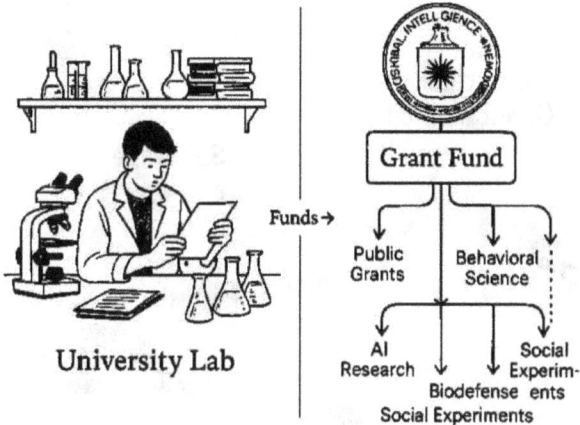

University Lab

Grant Fund

Funds →

Public Grants

Behavioral Science

AI Research

Biodefense

Social Experiments

Social Experiments

Case File: Operation Northwoods and "what might have been"

In 1962, America's Joint Chiefs of Staff drafted a plan so audacious it reads like pulp fiction: stage terror attacks on U.S. soil and blame Cuba to justify an invasion. Proposed tactics ranged from sinking a refugee boat to faking the shoot-down of a passenger jet, complete with a carefully planted debris field. President Kennedy's steadfast "no" consigned the memo to limbo, but its eventual declassification proves how close the world came to war by deception.

WHAT NORTHWOODS TAUGHT US

If a proposal reaches the president's desk, a culture capable of conceiving it already thrives in lower tiers.

JCS
13 March 1962

Since it woold seem.... However, these justifications for U.S. military intervention in Cuba, available
for our politics (and an actions for a positical Sub-

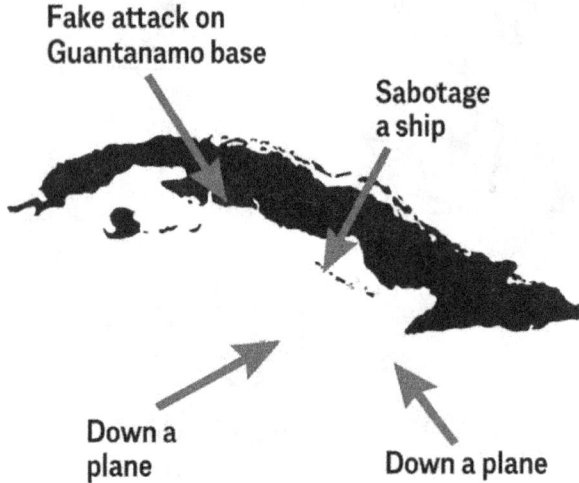

**Fake attack on
Guantanamo base**

**Sabotage
a ship**

**Down a
plane**

Down a plane

Operation Northwoods

Provocations Plan against Cuba

Patterns of Suppression: A Field Guide

Across continents and decades, agencies deploy the same four-step recipe:

1. **Delay:** Classify broadly, review rarely.

2. **Dilute:** Release only partial records; let absence breed confusion.

3. **Defame:** Dismiss early critics as fringe theorists.

4. **Delegate:** Outsource sensitive work to private contractors beyond FOIA reach.

When the truth finally surfaces, the responsible officers have retired, the statutory clock on prosecution has expired, and the narrative feels like ancient history.

Collateral Cases: When Secrets Imploded

- **Tuskegee Syphilis Study (1932-1972):** Public-health officials observed, but did not treat, infected Black men to chart disease progression. A whistle-blowing epidemiologist's conscience ended it after forty years.

- **COINTELPRO (1956-1971):** FBI operatives infiltrated civil-rights and anti-war groups, planting forged letters to spark internal rifts. Exposure arrived only when activists burglarized an FBI field office and leaked the files.

- **ECHELON & Five-Eyes (1947-present):** post-WW II signals-intelligence alliance vacuuming global communications. First hinted at by a classified UKUSA treaty, later acknowledged when investigative journalists traced satellite dishes across Yorkshire and the Australian outback.

The New York Times

PENTAGON PAPERS

June 13, 1971 —
Leaked Defense
Dept. study exposes
decades of hidden
Vietnam War
decisions.

The Washington Post

NSA SPY NETWORK

June 20, 2013
Barton Gellman
reveals mass
electronic
surveillance
programs.

The Guardian

GLOBAL SURVEILLANCE FILES

Nov 28, 2013 —
Edward Snowden
archive uncovers
international
spying.

Shattering Secrecy:
Landmark Press Exposés

Psychological Architecture of Secrecy

Why do agencies cling to secrets long after strategic value decays? Three forces dominate:

TRIGGER POINTS FOR DECLASSIFICATION

Death of the architect; regime change; lawsuit with discovery phase; competing leak that makes silence riskier than confession.

---

1. **Institutional Ego:** Prestige accrues to those who "know what others don't."

2. **Damage Anticipation:** Fear that public fury will dwarf the original wrongdoing.

3. **Control Momentum:** Once formed, a security apparatus grows like ivy—secrecy becomes both means and end.

This architecture yields a perverse irony: the longer knowledge is withheld, the more explosive its eventual release.

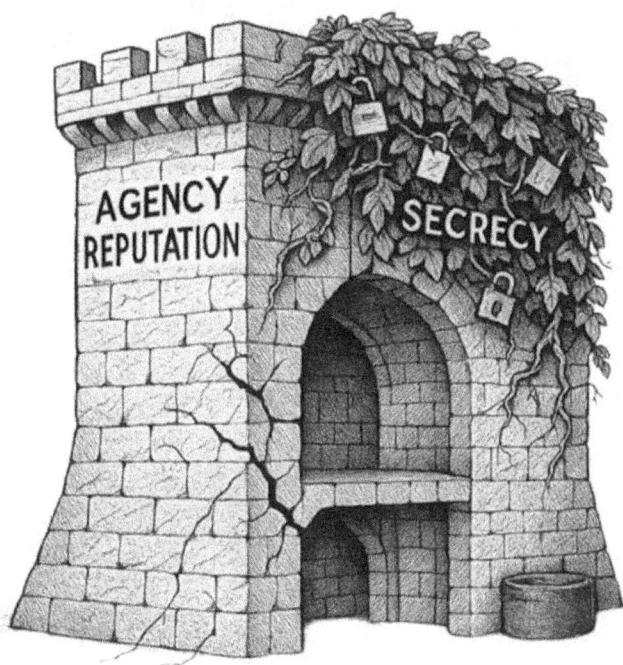

Fortified Façade: Agency Reputation under Scrutiny

Global Echoes: Secrecy Beyond U.S. Borders

- **Canada's MK-Ultra Twin:** Dr. Ewen Cameron's mind-wipe experiments, funded jointly by the CIA and Canadian government grants, show that secrecy is a transnational contagion.

- **Soviet Biopreparat (1973-1988):** A bioweapons megaplex masquerading as vaccine labs. Defector Ken Alibek's testimony revealed hidden anthrax factories after the USSR collapsed.

- **United Kingdom's Menwith Hill:** A rolling sea of radomes on Yorkshire moorland, officially "communications support." Parliamentary investigations exposed its role in global electronic eavesdropping.

- **Chile's Project FUBELT (1970-1973):** Covert U.S. operations to destabilize President Allende; documents surfaced decades later, confirming what Chileans had long suspected.

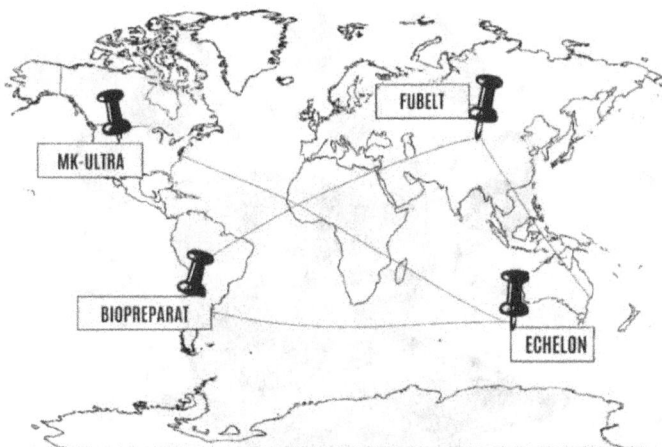

GLOBAL COVERT OPS NETWORK

Tools of the Twenty-First-Century Truth-Seeker

The era of bulky photocopiers has yielded to cloud drives and blockchain time stamps. Investigators now wield:

- **FOIA bots:** Automated scripts filing simultaneous requests across agencies.

- **Metadata forensics:** Reading edit history and GPS tags rescued from "sanitized" PDFs.

- **Crowdsourced cross-reference:** Distributed volunteers combing document dumps for "needle" phrases that link to undisclosed programs.

- **Secure drop-boxes:** Encryption-layered portals protecting whistle-blower anonymity while guaranteeing unaltered files.

SHATTERED SECRECY
DECRYPTING CLASSIFIED ARCHIVE

Operation Northwoods Revisited: A Counterfactual Lens

THE FOUR QUESTIONS EVERY NEW LEAK MUST ANSWER

1. *Authenticity: Can cryptographic hashes verify the file chain?*
2. *Context: Where does this fit within known operations?*
3. *Consequence: Who stands to gain—or lose—most?*
4. *Counter-narrative: How will agencies try to discredit the leak?*

Imagine the memo had been approved. Cuban refugees massacred at sea, a Miami shopping district bombed by "Castro agents," grieving families clamouring for swift retaliation. The Caribbean becomes a war zone, Soviet advisers pour in; nuclear brinkmanship escalates a year earlier than the real-world Missile Crisis. The takeaway: unexecuted conspiracies can still shape history by revealing how far strategists are willing to go.

Actual History
vs. *Northwoods Activated*

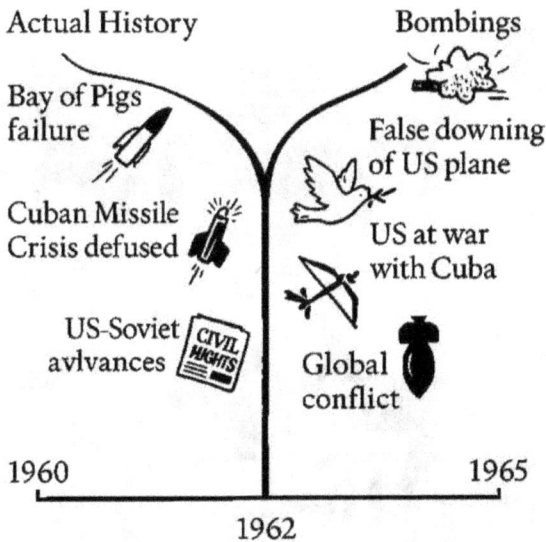

Actual History	Bombings
Bay of Pigs failure	False downing of US plane
Cuban Missile Crisis defused	US at war with Cuba
US-Soviet avlvances	Global conflict
1960	1965

1962

The Cost of Courage: Whistle-Blowers and Human Fallout

- **Daniel Ellsberg:** Branded a traitor for revealing Vietnam duplicity; decades later, hailed as a champion of transparency.

- **Dr. Jeffrey Wigand:** Exposed tobacco-industry perjury; silenced by lawsuits and smear campaigns.

- **Reality Winner & Edward Snowden:** Faced draconian charges under the Espionage Act—modern evidence that legal structures protect secrets better than they protect citizens.

The personal trajectories of these figures underscore a grim calculus: in the war between truth and state, the human cost is front-loaded onto the messenger.

Lessons from the Vault

1. **Secrecy Breeds Overreach.** When oversight is absent, experimental ethics drift from "Can we?" to "Why not?", evidenced by hallucinogenic interrogations and biological test aerosols sprayed over unsuspecting cities.

2. **Time Is a Solvent.** Every sealed archive decays under pressure from shifting administrations, aging participants, and evolving technology.

3. **Narrative Control Outlives the File.** Even when documents surface, spin-doctors frame them as "ancient history" or "necessary measures."

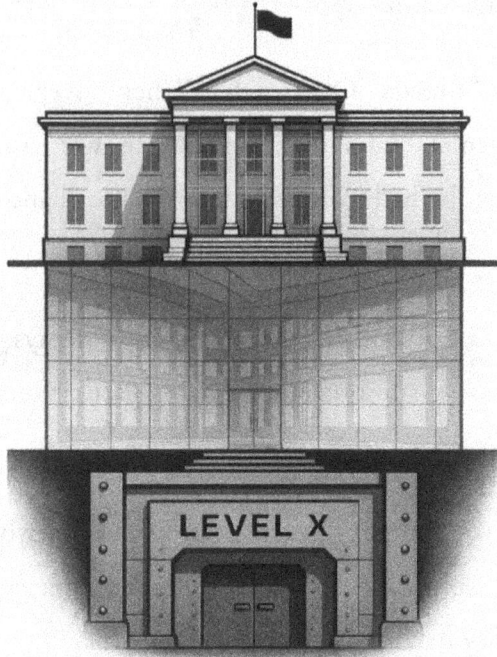

Beneath the Facade

Toolkit for the Reader-Investigator

THE PARADOX OF TRANSPARENCY

The more open a government appears, the more sophisticated its mechanisms for cloaking the few secrets that truly matter.

- **Archival Triangulation:** Compare identical documents released by different agencies; redaction patterns reveal priorities.

- **Budget Sleuthing:** Follow unexplained "black budget" line items across fiscal years; sudden jumps often coincide with covert expansions.

- **Interdisciplinary Cross-Check:** Pair security-state disclosures with seemingly unrelated scientific grants—sometimes the money trail is clearer than the memo trail.

- **Ethical Compass:** Pursue evidence, not ideology. Cognitive bias is the hidden ally of institutional secrecy.

FOLLOW
THE
MONEY
+METADATA

Closing Argument: Light as an Act of Will

Governments battling for truth suppression resemble medieval alchemists guarding formulas—yet the crucible of democracy demands a reverse transmutation: turning hidden lead into civic gold. Declassification is not a clerical act but a civil-rights victory scored one page at a time.

Whether dissecting MK-Ultra's pharmacological nightmares or Operation Northwoods' near-miss with manufactured terror, the lesson is consistent: *power does not concede facts willingly.* Every revelation has been purchased with sleepless nights, broken careers, or spilled blood.

You, reader, now possess the investigative grammar—FOIA petitions, metadata scrutiny, context triangulation—to advance the fight. The next vault may open because someone armed with this chapter's tools decides the truth can outbid fear.

Chapter 6

The Economics of Silence

How the world's fattest wallets keep the slimmest files, and why the price of energy is often the price of truth.

History loves to portray itself as an open ledger, but the ledgers that decide what gets written—and what gets burned—belong to treasuries, trusts, and transnational combines. From the gold-vault quiet of Swiss private banks to the scented suites where oil ministers sign night-time deals, money has the power to gag archives more effectively than any dictator. In this chapter, you will step inside that hush, armed with a single, dangerous question: **Who profits when knowledge disappears?**

How wealth and power bury inconvenient truths

When paleo historian Michael Cremo analysed 19th-century fossil reports, he noticed a pattern: anomalous finds that contradicted

---

THE KNOWLEDGE FILTER

Symptoms: hoax claims, accusations, journal rejections, career roadblocks.
Funding levers: endowments, strategic grants, industry sponsorships.
Net result: an "official" timeline that flatters power, not evidence.

evolutionary orthodoxy simply vanished from textbooks. He called this process the **knowledge filter**—a polite phrase for intellectual censorship powered by social prestige and research funding.

Money intensifies that filter. Laboratories rely on grants; universities rely on donors; journals rely on advertisers. A single petrochemical foundation or sovereign-wealth entity can starve uncomfortable research while feeding studies that reinforce its preferred narrative. "Credible knowledge," one reviewer of Cremo observed, is usually "situated at an intersection between physical locales and social distinctions." The polite translation: **follow the endowment, find the edit.**

The Invisible Hand's Darker Twins

Oil Cartels: How Scarcity is Engineered

From the 1928 Red Line Agreement to the OPEC price shocks of the 1970s, crude has been curated more than cultivated. Early "Seven Sisters" companies signed territorial pacts that limited drilling, throttled refinery capacity, and publicly justified price hikes as the *natural* response to scarcity, a scarcity they manufactured. Modern state producers replicate the tactic through export quotas: a few million withheld barrels can still finance entire propaganda arms and data analytics lobbies.

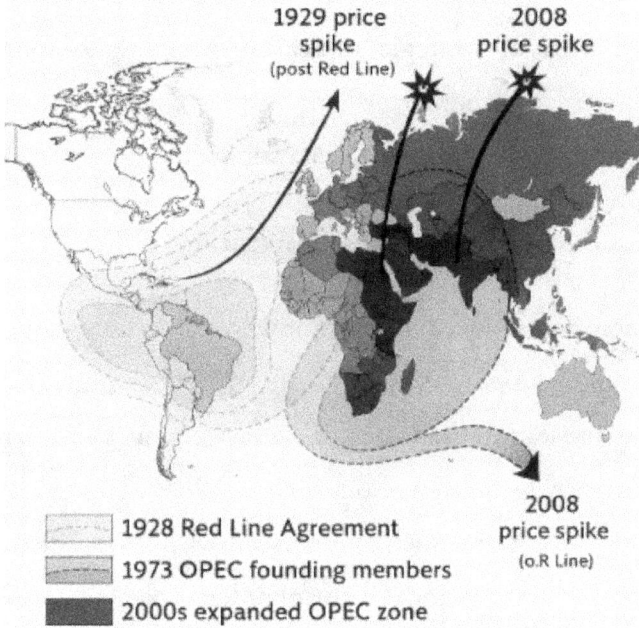

CARTEL SHADOWS: OIL PRICE SPIKES THROUGH THE CENTURY

1929 price spike (post Red Line)

2008 price spike

2008 price spike (o.R Line)

1928 Red Line Agreement

1973 OPEC founding members

2000s expanded OPEC zone

Banking Dynasties: Vaults as Black Holes

Oil determines who rules the pump; private banking decides who rules the archives. Consider the House of Rothschild, whose London headquarters—New Court—has quietly financed wars, railways, even governments, while guarding client correspondence in an inner sanctum nick-named "the Dead Letter Room."

Swiss partners such as Pictet & Cie and Lombard Odier protect fortunes behind unlimited-liability shells that virtually guarantee silence; litigation would mean ruin for the partners themselves, so they settle in shadows. German firms like Warburg & Co. and Oppenheim perfected the art of **strategic relocation**—moving headquarters or whole ledgers across borders when regimes changed, ensuring that inconvenient documents never meet a subpoena.

Case File – The Suppressed Invention of Free Energy

Every generation produces an inventor who claims to bypass the meter. In 1899, Nikola Tesla's Wardenclyffe prototype hinted at wireless power transmission; in the 1950s, T. Henry Moray's "Radiant Energy Device" allegedly lit bulbs without fuel; in 1985, Stanley Meyer drove a dune buggy on "water fuel." None secured mass production. Each faced patent seizures (national-security orders), mysterious lab fires, or lethal legal fees.

Cremo's research shows the template: first **ridicule the anomaly**, then **re-date or mis-label**, finally, **truncate** the record. The energy sector

THE BILDERBERG LEVER

Annual guest lists—bank chairs, energy CEOs, defence ministers—read like a merger between Wall Street and NATO. The meeting issues no minutes, yet participants routinely ascend to cabinet and central-bank posts within a political cycle.

adds a heavier tool—**buyout with gag clause.** If the creator signs, the tech is buried; if not, prosecution or bad-press storms follow.

Patent to Oblivion

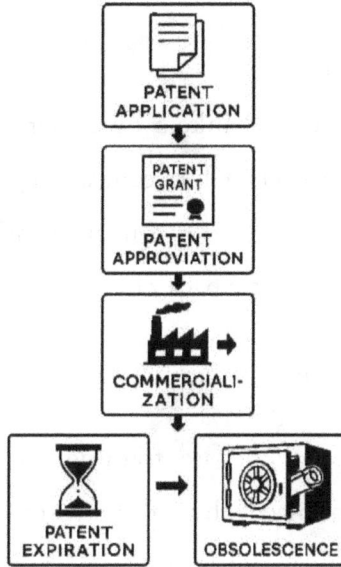

Patterns Of Economic Suppression

Data Gate-keeping

HOW TO BURY A PATENT

1. *File a notice of interest via a shell firm.*
2. *Offer a life-changing sum tied to perpetual NDA.*
3. *Classify key schematics under export-control regs.*
4. *Allow the rumor mill to brand the inventor a crank.*
5. *Re-file derivative patents in marginal jurisdictions to pre-empt rediscovery.*

Listening hubs like RAF Menwith Hill vacuum commercial phone traffic "for national security," but EU investigators have documented its use in corporate bidding wars, enabling favoured U.S. firms to undercut rivals by knowing their sealed numbers in advance.

Currency Leverage

Coutts & Co. ("the Queen's bankers") weathered 2008 partly because its clientele could move assets before central-bank policy shifts became public. Foreknowledge is a quieter cousin of insider trading—utterly legal if obtained via diplomatic back channels.

Media Endowment Echo

Think-tank grants dictate debate framing. A $5 million "energy-transition study" endowed by a petrostate seldom mentions decentralized solar cooperatives. The study circulates under a respected university imprint; journalists quote it; policymakers cite the journalists. The circle closes, and the cheaper reality stays unfunded.

Tools For the Truth-Seeker

1. **Audit the Funders** – Track who paid for the symposium, whose white paper just rewrote your history syllabus.

2. **Demand Raw Data** – If an archive refuses digitization, ask why; latent copyrights often mask embarrassment, not protection.

3. **Leverage Freedom-of-Information Lag** – In many jurisdictions, economic agreements older than 30 years lose confidentiality; schedule requests accordingly.

4. **Cross-Reference Patent Graveyards** – Compare abandoned patents with sudden corporate breakthroughs; gaps invite questions.

5. **Practice Epistemic Triangulation** – Pair establishment sources with outsider archives; the tension line often points to buried gold.

Truth-Seeker's Toolkit

FIVE FOUNDATIONS OF RELIABLE RESEARCH

Funding
Transparency

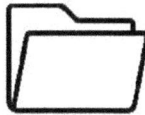

Open
Data Access

Timeless
Tracking

IP
clearance

IP
Clearance

Ethical
Navigation

Your electricity bill, your mortgage rate, your fuel gauge—each is a monthly memo from the Economics of Silence. The numbers rise or fall not merely on supply but on what has been *allowed* to become visible. As you venture deeper into these Dark Archives, remember: the loudest secrets are often the ones spoken in balance sheets, not in words. Challenge them, and you may find that "official history" is just an audited myth awaiting your signature on the next line.

Chapter 7

The VIP Ledger — The Epstein Files & the Myth of "The List"

The Rumour That Ate the Internet

It starts with a word that does more work than any PDF ever could: list.

A single noun hints at order, authority, certainty — and the promise that, somewhere, there's a clean roster of villains. For years, social feeds and late-night group chats have spoken of an "Epstein client list," a definitive ledger that would implicate the famous and powerful in sex trafficking.

Here is the first plain fact of this chapter: **there is no official, single "client list."** That's not interpretation; that's what the record shows. What exists are *discrete categories of documents* — flight logs, address books, travel schedules, depositions, exhibits, and court filings — produced across multiple cases and years, often for different purposes and gathered under different evidentiary standards. When a federal court unsealed **Giuffre v. Maxwell** materials in early January 2024,

> *When someone says "the list," ask: Which document type? What was its purpose? Who created it, and why? If they can't answer, you're being sold a slogan, not a source.*

many headlines and posts called it "the list," but the documents were a mixed set: correspondence, exhibits, and references to people in roles ranging from witnesses to lawyers to alleged victims. Being *named* in those filings did **not** equal an accusation of a crime.

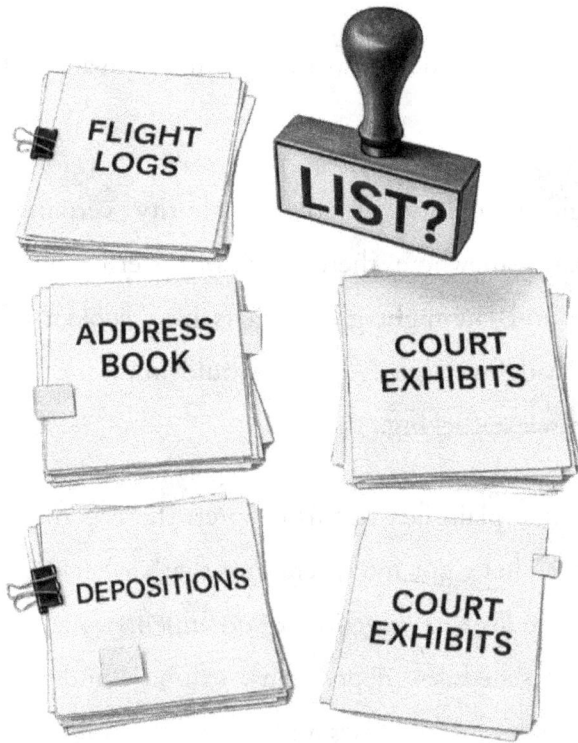

No 'List' - Separate Records
Flight logs, address book, depositions, and exhibits

A Map of the Real Files (What They Are — and aren't)

Flight Logs (Pilot Manifests).

Pilots kept passenger manifests recording who flew on which legs and when. They are transportation records, not verdicts. They establish proximity and movement — *who* traveled *with whom, on which date, between which airports.* They do not, by themselves, prove criminal activity.

The Address Book (The "Black Book").

An address book is a contact list — a Rolodex of social, professional, and service connections: numbers, emails, sometimes notes. Journalists published a redacted copy years ago; it contains hundreds of entries, many of which were never accused of any wrongdoing. A contact entry is not evidence of a crime.

Calendars & Schedules (Post-Conviction Networking).

Investigative reporting later surfaced calendars and emails from the 2010s showing meetings Epstein sought with academics, executives, and officials *after* his 2008 state plea. These are meeting notes, not charging documents, and they are relevant primarily to mapping networks — not to proving specific offenses.

Depositions & Civil Filings (2015–2017, Unsealed 2024).

The 2024 unsealing in *Giuffre v. Maxwell* released hundreds of pages from a **defamation** case. Those materials mention ~150+ people in all kinds of roles — alleged victims, journalists, lawyers, social acquaintances, and more. Courts and reputable outlets stressed that these were *case documents,* not an official roster of "clients."

Criminal Case Filings (2019 SDNY).

In July 2019, federal prosecutors in the Southern District of New York charged Epstein with sex trafficking of minors. He died the following month; the case was dismissed after a hearing at which the victims spoke. These filings and press releases are the authoritative record of the federal case posture.

Maxwell's Prosecution & Sentencing (2021–2022).

Epstein's associate was convicted in 2021 and sentenced to 20 years in 2022 for conspiring with him to sexually abuse minors — another anchor point confirming the trafficking scheme without creating a magical "list."

Know Your Docs:
What It Is / What Is'n't

Flight Itinerary
✓ route & dates from airline or agent
✗ not a ticket or boarding pass

Proof of Address
✓ utility bill or bank statement
  showing your name & address
✗ not your contacts list or profile bio

Appointment Confirmation
✓ official email/letter with time,
  date, location & reference
✗ not a calendar hold you made yourself

Court Order
✓ signed, stamped order from a court
✗ not a lawyer's letter or allegation

Official Transcript
✓ registrar-issued record of
  courses & grades
✗ not a diploma or CV

How the "List" Myth Took Over

Phase 1 — Compression: social media collapses complex archives into one easy word: *list.*

Phase 2 — Conflation: Flight logs + address book + deposition screenshots are pasted into a single collage and captioned "clients."

Phase 3 — Circulation: Memes outrun corrections; nuance loses to virality.

Phase 4 — Clarification: Courts and major outlets clarify that unsealed documents are not a client roster; fact-checkers debunk virals. In January 2024, as the first batch of *Giuffre v. Maxwell* filings came out, accurate explainers emphasized: these were **not** a canon of "clients," and many people named were neither accused nor suspected of crimes. That framing has been repeatedly reiterated by AP, PBS, and others.

The Social Blender

PDF   Social   Client List

Compression creates fiction

What Changed in 2025 (and What Didn't)?

In mid-2025, the U.S. Justice Department publicly stated that it had **no "client list"** to release and that its review found **no such master ledger** — a notable, on-the-record clarification that punctured years of rumour.

Separately, congressional pressure has pushed for broader disclosures of investigative files (with victim redactions), and senior lawmakers have said DOJ document production to committees would begin — a procedural development, not a validation of a mythical list. The scope and public availability of any such productions remain unclear.

When you hear "the files are coming Friday," ask: *Which files, to whom, under what subpoena, with what redactions?* "Production" isn't the same as "publication."

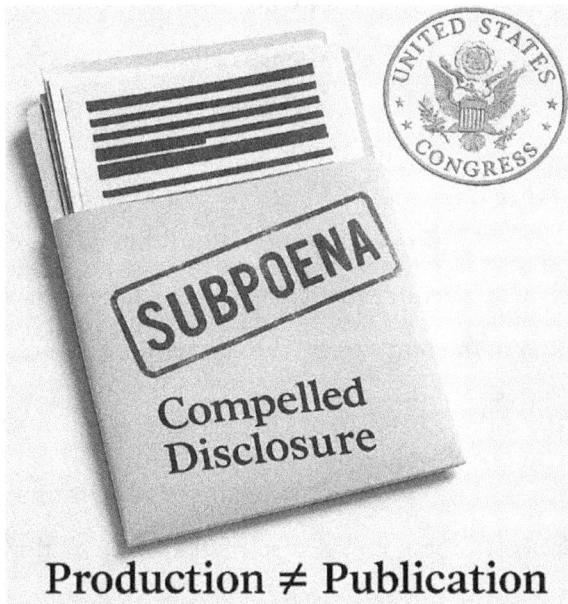

Production ≠ Publication

The Two Presidents (By Number, Not Name)

Two U.S. presidents appear in this document universe. We will use office numbers only. We will also separate verified facts from online embellishments.

The 42nd U.S. President

What the documents show:

- The 42nd president **flew multiple times** on Epstein-owned aircraft in 2002–2003 on foundation-related international trips. His office publicly described those flights as **four trips** (one to Europe, one to Asia, and two to Africa) with staff, supporters, and Secret Service aboard.
- There is **no evidence** he visited Epstein's private island; **none of the available flight logs** list him on Virgin Islands–bound legs. That remains the consensus of independent fact-checking.

What the documents do *not* show:

- They do not prove that the 42nd knew of, endorsed, or participated in Epstein's crimes. No charges have been filed against him in connection with Epstein. (If that changes, you'll see it in formal filings — not memes.)

When a claim resurfaces ("He went to the island 28 times"), can you trace it to a docket, a log, or a press release? If not, it's not evidence.

The 45th U.S. President (then a private citizen)

What the documents show:

- Flight logs include the 45th as a passenger on at least **one flight in January 1997** (Palm Beach → Newark). That comes from logs unsealed years ago in civil litigation.

What the documents do *not* show:

- As with the 42nd, logs do not show the 45th flying to Epstein's Island, and no charges have been filed against him in connection with Epstein. (Flight logs are movement records, not criminal findings.)

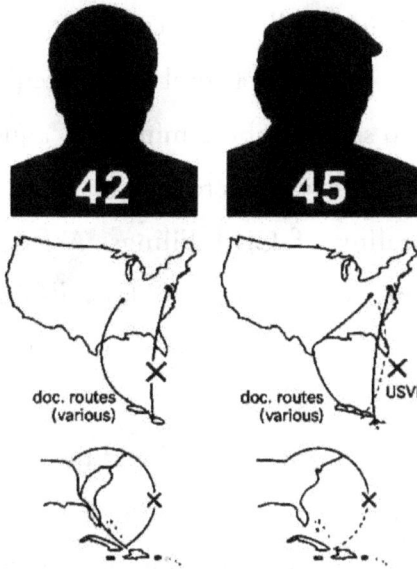

What the logs actually show

Based on publicly released Epstein pilot logs (David Rodgers) through 2025: no entries show flights by 42 or 45 to U.S. Virgin Islands.

The Core Case, in Brief (So We Stay Oriented)

- **2008 Florida Non-Prosecution Agreement (NPA).** Epstein avoided federal charges via a controversial NPA negotiated by the U.S. Attorney in South Florida, pleading to state charges and serving a short county sentence with work release. A 2020 DOJ review criticized **"poor judgment"** in that resolution and victim notification failures, while concluding prosecutors didn't commit chargeable professional misconduct.

- **2019 SDNY Indictment.** Federal prosecutors in New York charged Epstein with sex trafficking of minors; he was detained pending trial and died by suicide a month later.

- **2021–2022 Maxwell Conviction & Sentence.** Epstein's associate was convicted at trial and sentenced to 20 years for conspiring to sexually abuse minors — a judicial finding that the trafficking scheme was real and criminal.

- **2024 Unsealing of Civil Filings.** A federal judge ordered identities unsealed in *Giuffre v. Maxwell* filings; the documents were evidence in a defamation case, not a criminal list of "clients."

- **2025 DOJ Clarification.** DOJ said there is **no "client list"** to release. Political committees continue to seek documents; any public releases will be redacted to protect victims.

Epstein Case Timeline: 2008–2025

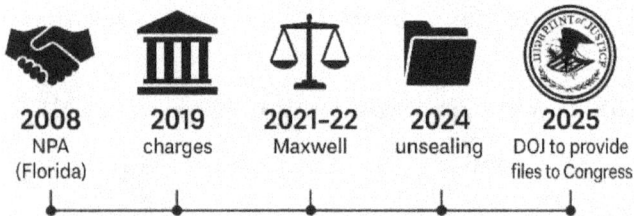

2008	2019	2021-22	2024	2025
NPA (Florida)	charges	Maxwell	unsealing	DOJ to provide files to Congress

Flight Logs, Up Close: What Can You Prove with a Manifest?

What a log can prove:

- A person's presence on a plane for a given leg on a given date.
- The route (origin/destination), aircraft tail number, and sometimes seat notes.

What a log cannot prove:

- Why a passenger flew.
- What they knew, believed, or did before/after.
- Criminal conduct — unless corroborated by other evidence.

Crowds online often treat a pilot's manifest as a bill of indictment. It's not. It is meaningful — proximity matters in conspiracy cases — but it is **not** dispositive on its own. The unredacted logs circulating publicly show dozens of high-profile names across years, routes, and contexts; they are a *starting point* for questions, not an end.

The Address Book (and Why Contacts Are Not Crimes)

Epstein's so-called "black book" is a contacts list. In 2015, a redacted copy was posted online; it reads exactly like what it is — entries on hundreds of people: captains of industry, journalists, artists, academics, service providers, and friends. The presence of a name in a contact book shows a social or professional connection (or even just an introduction), not guilt. If you want to understand **power**, address books are revealing. If you want to prove a **crime**, you need more than a phone number.

What the 2024 Unsealed Materials Contain

The 2024 unsealing in *Giuffre v. Maxwell* released nearly a thousand pages in waves. Inside: deposition excerpts, motions, and references to people in varied contexts (attempted subpoenas, background mentions, media inquiries, etc.). Several outlets stressed — prominently — that the papers were **not** a definitive "client list," and that many names were already known or were **not accused of misconduct.** That is the contemporary consensus among serious reporting and fact-checking.

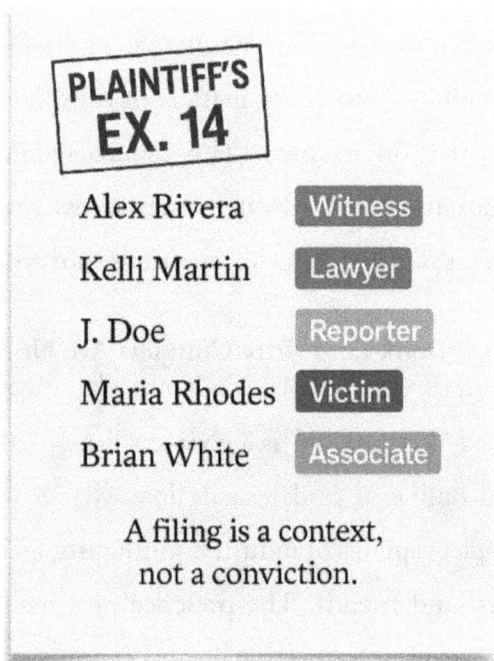

PLAINTIFF'S
EX. 14

Alex Rivera	Witness
Kelli Martin	Lawyer
J. Doe	Reporter
Maria Rhodes	Victim
Brian White	Associate

A filing is a context,
not a conviction.

Your Field Kit for Reading the Epstein Dossiers (Without Getting Worked)

1. **Identify the Doc Type.** Log? Address book? Deposition? Filing? Press release? (Your standard of inference should match.)

2. **Trace to Source.** Screenshot → docket number → exhibit → full PDF. If you can't trace it, treat it as a rumor.

3. **Separate *Mention* from *Allegation*.** Many 2024 documents list individuals as context, not suspects.

4. **Cross-Check Against Known Facts.** Maxwell's conviction establishes a trafficking enterprise. Logs establish travel. Don't let one stand in for the other.

5. **Note Redactions and Privacy Law.** Victim identities are protected; public productions will remain redacted.

Take any viral name + "Epstein list" claim. Can you find it in a court file? If yes, what *role* is that person in? If no, why was it so easy to share and so hard to source?

The Economics of Confusion

Why does the "list" myth persist? Because **ambiguity monetizes.** Screenshots are fast; archives are slow. One word ("list") outperforms four categories ("logs, contacts, calendars, filings"). Even without censorship, the public can be **misled by abundance** — a form of suppression by noise rather than by deletion.

Case Study: One Meme vs. the Record

The Meme: "The 42nd U.S. President went to the island 28 times."

The Record: Fact-checkers find *no evidence* of any such trips. Flight logs list many legs in 2002–2003 for humanitarian travel; **none** show a Virgin Islands destination with him aboard. His office has publicly denied any island visit.

The Meme: "The 45th U.S. President never had anything to do with Epstein."

The Record: Flight logs show at least one flight (Palm Beach → Newark, Jan. 1997). Proximity is recorded; criminal conduct is **not** established by that log.

If two claims can't survive a check against two public documents, why are they spreading? Who benefits from your confusion?

Why This Chapter?

You've already met three classic levers of suppression: ridicule, reinterpretation, and removal. The Epstein archive adds a fourth: **recomposition** — slicing, blending, and remaking documents into a simple, shareable fiction. The risk isn't merely reputational for the famous; it's moral for the survivors. When discourse chases a phantom "list," oxygen is pulled from the very things that *are* documented: grooming patterns, recruitment pipelines, and protection failures that let a predator operate.

What We Can Say — With Confidence

- Epstein ran a criminal enterprise that exploited minors; this is established by the federal indictment (2019) and by the 2021 guilty verdict against his associate.
- The 2024 unsealed civil filings were not a "client list" and included many names in non-accusatory contexts.
- The Justice Department has stated it has no "client list" to release; congressional committees continue to seek documents with redactions to protect victims.
- The 42nd president took documented trips on Epstein's planes (2002–2003), and there is **no evidence** he visited the island; the 45th took at least one 1997 flight. Flight logs show travel, not guilt.

EXHIBIT —
ESTABLISHED BY RECORD

- Epstein ran a criminal enterprise that exploited minors; this is established by the federal indictment (2019) and by the 2021 guilty verdict against his associate.
- The 2024 unsealed civil filings were not a "client list" and included many names in non-accusatory contexts.
- The Justice Department has stated it has no "client list" to release; congressional committees continue to seek documents with redactions to protect victims.
- The 42nd president took documented trips on Epstein's planes (2002–2003), and there is no evidence he visited the island; the 45th took at least one 1997 flight. Flight logs show travel.

Sources: DOJ SDNY press releases (2018, 2021); AP/PBS 2024–2025, FactCheck org; Business Insider

ESTABLISHED BY RECORD

What We Cannot Say (and Won't Pretend To)

- We cannot elevate a collage of screenshots into an evidentiary "list."
- We cannot turn a contact entry into a charge.
- We cannot know what is sealed to protect victims until it is lawfully unsealed.

- We cannot trade the boredom of real documents for the thrill of a single answer — not without lying to ourselves.

This chapter is not about clearing reputations or damning them by proximity. It's about **standing inside the archive** and asking it to speak for itself. The *documents we have* — criminal filings, sentencing records, flight logs, contact lists, depositions — tell a story that is large and ugly enough without embroidery. The 2019 indictment and the 2021 conviction confirm a sex-trafficking scheme. The 2024 unsealed civil filings add names and texture, not a ledger of "clients." The 2025 DOJ statement adds a final, uncomfortable clarity: **the tidy "list" the internet promised was never there.**

Which do you trust more: a one-word meme, or the messier, slower, documented truth?

Part III: The Archives They Don't Want You to See

Chapter 8: Disinformation & the Control of History

THE PRESS OF POWER

The Anatomy of Historical Manipulation

It has often been said that truth is the first casualty of war. But history itself is the long-term victim, carefully sculpted by those who wield power, not just victors on the battlefield, but gatekeepers within institutions of influence. What we call "official history" is a carefully maintained illusion, upheld by a powerful network of academia, governments, media conglomerates, and religious establishments. These entities, consciously or otherwise, enforce a carefully engineered consensus that becomes the definitive narrative for generations.

To question this narrative is to risk ridicule or worse. Yet, beneath the surface lies a vast underworld of evidence—classified files, hushed whistleblowers, redacted reports—that collectively reveal the hidden fingerprints of historical manipulation.

How propaganda becomes permanent history

Propaganda is not a recent phenomenon. From Roman emperors to modern intelligence agencies, disinformation has been systematically deployed to ensure compliance, control perception, and rewrite inconvenient truths. In our age of digital interconnectedness, the power of propaganda has not diminished—it has evolved. The lie, once disseminated through printed leaflets or word of mouth, now spreads

HISTORY AS PROPAGANDA:

History books are not merely records of the past; they are powerful instruments of propaganda, designed to shape collective memory and maintain existing power structures. This is why challenging historical narratives often triggers fierce resistance from established authorities.

instantaneously across digital platforms, solidifying into a historical "fact" overnight.

We believe our history to be objective, yet often it is simply the loudest voice or the most persistent repetition that determines what future generations will regard as truth. History is a weaponized form of memory, selectively curated, edited, and preserved to serve powerful interests.

Channels of Persuasion:
A Timeline of propaganda tools

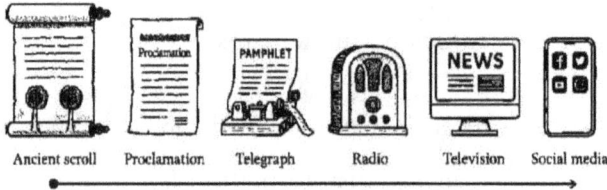

| Ancient scroll | Proclamation | Telegraph | Radio | Television | Social media |

A Timeline of propaganda tools

Why whistleblowers are silenced

REPETITION IS TRUTH:

"Repeat a lie often enough, and it becomes the truth." This principle, attributed to Joseph Goebbels, reveals precisely how propaganda transforms transient falsehoods into enduring historical myths.

Whistle-blowers are the truth's last line of defence against the erasure machine of official history. But they are frequently vilified, persecuted, or silenced because their revelations threaten the carefully woven narratives supporting existing structures of power. These courageous insiders embody the profound moral responsibility of bringing hidden truths to public awareness, knowing fully that their actions carry enormous personal risk.

From Daniel Ellsberg's Pentagon Papers revealing the hidden horrors of Vietnam to Edward Snowden's exposure of pervasive digital surveillance, whistleblowers have reshaped history by forcibly injecting suppressed realities into public consciousness. Yet their voices are often quickly drowned out, their reputations dismantled, and their evidence discredited by a system desperate to preserve its narrative coherence.

The retaliation against whistleblowers serves a chilling purpose: to discourage future truth-tellers from stepping forward.

Case File: The Missing JFK Assassination Records

WHY THEY FEAR WHISTLEBLOWERS:

Whistleblowers expose more than just facts—they reveal systemic corruption, hypocrisy, and deception at the heart of trusted institutions. They disrupt carefully constructed historical narratives, prompting dangerous questions.

If history were truly transparent, one would expect an event as thoroughly scrutinized as the assassination of President John F. Kennedy to have no lingering mysteries. Yet decades after that fateful day in Dallas on November 22, 1963, thousands of government files remain sealed or heavily redacted, creating fertile ground for suspicion and conspiracy.

The official version, the Warren Commission Report, presents a tidy narrative: Lee Harvey Oswald, acting alone, fired three shots from a sixth-floor window of the Texas School Book Depository. Yet public Skepticism has endured precisely because critical records—CIA operations, FBI surveillance data, and detailed intelligence reports— remain buried deep in classified vaults. Each passing deadline for the release of these records fuels suspicion that the truth is intentionally obscured.

Uncovering these files is not simply a matter of historical curiosity; it is essential for understanding the hidden dynamics of power within American governance. The continued suppression of JFK records

WHY JFK STILL MATTERS:

Releasing the hidden JFK files could not only rewrite history but might also dismantle enduring public trust in governmental institutions. Keeping these files secret has arguably done more to fuel conspiratorial thinking than transparency ever could.

implies far more than mere bureaucratic inertia—it suggests active concealment of truths too disruptive to acknowledged narratives.

The Knowledge Filter: Gatekeeping Historical Reality

The shaping of history relies heavily on the phenomenon of the "knowledge filter," a systemic process where information conflicting with accepted doctrines is quietly discarded, suppressed, or discredited. It operates in education, publishing, journalism, and even entertainment. Textbooks subtly omit uncomfortable episodes;

academic papers challenging orthodox views rarely pass peer review; documentaries questioning official narratives find little mainstream distribution.

These filters are often enforced unconsciously by individuals trained to recognize "acceptable" knowledge. But sometimes, the filtering is deliberate and overt, driven by political expediency or corporate agendas. The resulting cultural amnesia obscures our collective past, constraining our ability to learn from history's full complexity.

When Conspiracy Theories Become Conspiracy Facts

Today's widely acknowledged historical scandals were yesterday's ridiculed conspiracy theories. MK-Ultra, Operation Northwoods, COINTELPRO—all initially dismissed as paranoid fantasies, until brave individuals or accidental disclosures confirmed their existence. This raises a troubling question: how many other conspiracies, now casually derided, await future validation?

Recognizing genuine conspiracies requires careful discernment: balancing Skepticism with openness, verification with vigilance. Discrediting all claims as conspiracy theories risks complicity in maintaining ignorance, while accepting all claims uncritically is equally dangerous. The critical investigator walks a razor's edge, armed with patience, intellectual humility, and rigorous evidence-based analysis.

Digital Amnesia and the Future of Historical Truth

The digital age promised greater access to information, but paradoxically, it has intensified the battle over historical truth. Online archives can vanish overnight; search results can be algorithmically manipulated; and social media platforms can invisibly bury controversial content. The mechanisms for historical suppression have evolved—no longer limited to locked cabinets and censored textbooks but embedded into algorithms, terms of service, and digital erasure.

Ensuring historical transparency today requires new investigative skills: digital forensics, metadata analysis, blockchain archiving, and decentralized storage solutions. Tomorrow's historians will face unprecedented challenges and unprecedented opportunities to rescue suppressed truths from digital oblivion.

DISMISSING THE TRUTH:

Governments and institutions frequently label inconvenient truths as "conspiracy theories," precisely because such terms carry built-in ridicule, effectively neutralizing dissent.

Your role, dear reader, is critical: remain vigilant, sceptical, and insatiably curious. Understand that history is not static—it is contested territory. Those who control the historical narrative shape society's collective identity, morality, and destiny. Uncovering hidden truths is not merely about revising textbooks; it's about reclaiming our right to understand reality in all its uncomfortable complexity.

History is far too important to leave to official narratives alone.

Chapter 9

Ancient Myths, Modern Secrets

When folklore is encoded truth

Our histories, both individual and collective, are shaped by narratives. Yet, curiously enough, humanity often relegates some of its oldest, most potent stories to the realm of mere myth, folklore, or fantasy. Official history textbooks offer neatly packaged timelines, carefully curated to fit prevailing paradigms. But beneath these sanitized accounts lie deeper, darker archives— repositories of truths so potent they threaten established beliefs, ideologies, and power structures. In these dark archives reside myths, legends, and oral traditions that stubbornly persist through millennia, hinting at forbidden knowledge hidden just beneath the surface of civilization.

It is a curious irony that stories we dismiss as fanciful today were often once revered as sacred truths. Such myths were not merely entertaining or moralistic fables—they were often sophisticated vehicles of encoded knowledge. Folklore, mythology, and sacred texts served as vessels carrying critical information about natural disasters, lost civilizations, cosmic phenomena, and even warnings of future cataclysms.

Veiled Truths: The Storyteller's Shadow

Flood Myths, Lost Continents, and Forbidden Timelines

Perhaps the most widespread and enduring myths across global cultures are those of the Great Flood. From Mesopotamia's epic of Gilgamesh to the biblical deluge of Noah, from India's ancient texts

MYTH AS MEMORY

Many ancient myths were not just symbolic allegories but encoded historical records. Passed down orally over generations, these stories protected critical knowledge through metaphor and allegory, shielding them from erasure by conquerors and religious authorities.

recounting Manu's ark to Indigenous American flood stories, the ubiquity of such accounts raises unsettling questions.

Could these stories of devastating floods, found independently in distant cultures separated by oceans and continents, reflect a shared historical memory rather than mere coincidence?

The universality of flood myths has led many truth-seekers to speculate about catastrophic geological events erased from conventional history. Among these suppressed stories are legends of lost continents—Lemuria, Mu, and most famously, Atlantis—once thriving civilizations erased overnight by cataclysm. Official history discredits these as fantasies, yet the astonishing consistency of these myths across continents demands deeper scrutiny.

Recent scientific discoveries hint at reality beneath these dismissed narratives. Underwater ruins found in the Atlantic near the Azores and submerged structures off the coast of Japan (Yonaguni) resonate hauntingly with Plato's descriptions of Atlantis and other ancient narratives of lost civilizations. These discoveries, consistently

THE UNIVERSAL FLOOD

Nearly every culture on Earth recounts a devastating flood. Scientific evidence increasingly aligns with these myths, pointing toward global geological events at the end of the last Ice Age. Official history, however, remains reluctant to acknowledge such evidence, preferring neat linear timelines over chaotic truths.

underreported or ignored by mainstream academics, suggest hidden timelines of human civilization stretching much further back than officially sanctioned chronologies.

Heracleion: Echoes Beneath the Waves

Case File: Göbekli Tepe and the Rewriting of Civilization

Among the strongest pieces of evidence challenging orthodox historical timelines is the archaeological site known as Göbekli Tepe in modern-day Turkey. Discovered in the late 20th century and fully excavated only recently, Göbekli Tepe has shaken the foundations of accepted human history.

This sprawling, sophisticated complex of stone circles, intricately carved pillars, and monumental architecture was constructed around 9600 BCE, over 6,000 years before Stonehenge and the Great Pyramid of Giza. At this time, conventional historical doctrine insists humanity existed solely as hunter-gatherers, incapable of large-scale, organized projects. Yet, Göbekli Tepe stands defiantly, its mere existence an open rebellion against traditional archaeological consensus.

How can conventional timelines survive this profound challenge? They survive, it appears, only through strategic neglect. Göbekli Tepe's revolutionary implications have been downplayed or politely ignored by many mainstream historians and archaeologists. Its sophisticated astronomical alignments, intricate artistry, and sheer size strongly indicate that advanced, organized societies existed millennia earlier than previously thought possible.

Göbekli Tepe's stone pillars bear enigmatic carvings of animals, celestial motifs, and unknown symbols, seemingly encoding astronomical knowledge and possibly even preserving warnings of past cataclysms. Some scholars speculate that the complex served as a cosmic observatory or a sanctuary for survivors of a global disaster. Whatever its original purpose, Göbekli Tepe undeniably stands as a

GÖBEKLI TEPE: THE MONUMENT THAT SHOULDN'T EXIST

Göbekli Tepe is not merely a curiosity—it is a direct contradiction of the conventional historical narrative. Its existence compels a radical rewriting of the story of human civilization, which powerful academic institutions remain unwilling or unable to undertake.

testament to a forgotten age of civilization, forcing a reconsideration of humanity's timeline and capabilities.

Its intentional burial thousands of years ago further adds to the mystery. Why would ancient peoples deliberately conceal such an extraordinary monument? Perhaps to preserve crucial knowledge through cycles of disaster and societal collapse—an encoded message sent forward in time, waiting patiently beneath layers of earth for humanity to rediscover its forgotten heritage.

Göbekli Tepe: Celestial Temple at Dawn

Why These Truths Remain Hidden

Why, then, do such remarkable discoveries languish in obscurity or outright suppression? The answer lies in the entrenched resistance of established power structures—academic, religious, and political—to paradigm shifts. Official histories form foundational myths that reinforce cultural identities, religious beliefs, and institutional authority. Threatening these accepted narratives, whether intentionally or unintentionally, endangers the legitimacy of existing institutions and the power wielded by their gatekeepers.

The revelations contained in places like Göbekli Tepe, submerged ancient ruins, and global myths of cataclysmic floods compel uncomfortable questions. If humanity's true history is longer and richer than we have been allowed to believe, what other inconvenient truths lie hidden beneath official narratives? Perhaps ancient civilizations possessed knowledge and technology surpassing our own in certain aspects. Acknowledging this possibility undermines modern beliefs in perpetual progress and the superiority of contemporary societies.

Unlocking the Archives of the Mind

By confronting these suppressed truths, we unlock not just physical archives but the archives of our collective memory. Every lost story rediscovered, every suppressed artifact unearthed, brings us closer to understanding humanity's real origins and potential. The mythologies we once dismissed as mere superstition become invaluable guides, pointing toward hidden truths that institutional histories cannot—or will not—reveal.

This chapter invites you to reconsider myths not as primitive attempts at understanding the world, but as sophisticated, encoded repositories of real historical events. In embracing the legitimacy of these stories, we reclaim the narrative from institutions determined to shape it. By reopening the Dark Archives, we illuminate truths powerful enough to rewrite our collective identity and reshape the very foundations of what we call history.

THE POWER OF HISTORICAL AMNESIA

Institutional power thrives on historical amnesia. Keeping humanity unaware of its true past allows established systems to maintain control over society's trajectory, defining acceptable limits of knowledge and belief.

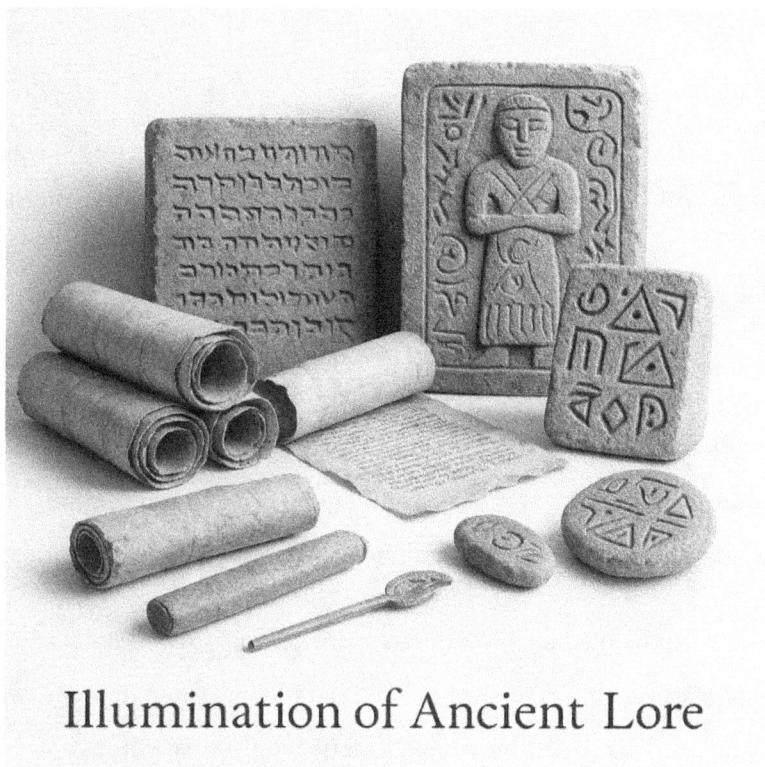

Illumination of Ancient Lore

You stand now at the threshold of revelation. The question remains—will you step through?

Chapter 10

The Digital Black Vault

Modern Censorship and the Battle for Information Control

*I*nformation is not merely power—it is the foundational currency of control. From ancient monarchs burning inconvenient manuscripts to modern corporations subtly editing Wikipedia pages, the impulse to suppress truth has adapted and evolved—but never vanished. Today's vaults are digital, their guardians invisible, their methods stealthy yet astonishingly potent.

Never before in human history has information flowed so freely, nor been controlled so aggressively. This paradox defines our era, where every digital fingerprint becomes evidence and every voice risks being silenced by algorithms and cyber warfare. In our supposedly transparent world, the true corridors of power lie hidden behind endless strings of code.

The digital black vault is not just metaphorical—it is real, active, and far-reaching. It is a system built by governments, corporations, and powerful interests, designed meticulously to filter reality before it ever

> *The truth is no longer simply hidden—it's algorithmically demoted, digitally quarantined, or silently erased by powerful gatekeepers who decide what deserves to be remembered and what must vanish.*

reaches your eyes. The gatekeepers who guard this vault aren't librarians or archivists, but coders and algorithms, serving agendas we may never fully grasp.

The Rise of Leaks, Hacks, and Anonymous Whistleblowers's

In response to this unprecedented censorship, a new breed of digital rebels has emerged. Anonymous whistleblowers, shadowy hackers, and underground leakers represent a counterforce pushing back against the digital gatekeepers. Their weapons are transparency, encryption, and anonymity; their targets are classified databases, secret communications, and hidden truths.

Platforms like WikiLeaks represent a seismic shift in the information war—a movement toward radical transparency. These groups see themselves not as criminals, but as guardians of democracy, freedom, and truth in an age of systematic deceit. They wage their battles anonymously, fully aware that exposure could lead to imprisonment, exile, or worse.

The stakes couldn't be higher. Governments and powerful institutions respond by tightening their digital chokeholds, passing draconian laws, expanding surveillance networks, and deploying increasingly sophisticated countermeasures to silence dissent.

Yet, despite these formidable odds, whistleblowers persist. Their actions remind us that truth can never be fully suppressed—those secrets have an innate drive toward the surface.

Veiled Messengers: Anonymity Unleashed

Case File: WikiLeaks and the Price of Exposure

Among the modern age's most controversial and consequential leaks is

> *Whistleblowers are modern prophets of inconvenient truths, risking everything to expose realities that powerful institutions would prefer to be buried.*

WikiLeaks. Founded on the radical idea that transparency can hold power accountable, WikiLeaks transformed the landscape of journalism, geopolitics, and public trust forever.

From the release of Collateral Murder footage showing American soldiers gunning down civilians, to the disclosure of sensitive diplomatic cables that exposed governmental duplicity worldwide, WikiLeaks forced open the digital black vault for public scrutiny.

But with these revelations came severe consequences. Julian Assange, the enigmatic face of WikiLeaks, became a global pariah, forced into exile, then imprisonment, relentlessly pursued by the very powers whose secrets he exposed. Chelsea Manning, the U.S. Army analyst who leaked the Collateral Murder footage and classified diplomatic cables, spent years behind bars, subjected to harsh conditions aimed at deterring future whistleblowers.

The message sent to would-be leakers was clear: reveal our secrets, and we will destroy you.

Yet WikiLeaks ignited a firestorm of awareness, inspiring a global conversation about the morality of state secrecy, the limits of power, and the essential nature of transparency to democracy.

The revelations exposed corruption, hypocrisy, and abuses of power on a scale never before imagined. They demonstrated conclusively that what is labeled "classified" often serves to hide wrongdoing rather than protect genuine national security.

SHADOWS OF POWER:
ASSANGE BEHIND BARS

The Digital Battlefield: Algorithms as Censors

Today, censorship is subtle yet more insidious than ever, driven by algorithms designed not only to silence but to shape the reality we perceive. Search engines and social media companies openly acknowledge using algorithms to demote or bury information they deem inappropriate, dangerous, or simply inconvenient.

The persecution of Julian Assange and Chelsea Manning exemplifies the real cost of exposing suppressed truths. Their treatment sends a chilling warning: step into the light, and you risk annihilation.

This new reality creates an illusion of openness—after all, the information still exists online—but it is buried beneath layers of digital obscurity, effectively erased from public consciousness. Such methods make active suppression unnecessary. Why delete when you can simply hide in plain sight?

From controversial medical research to political dissent, countless stories have been quietly erased from mainstream visibility. Algorithms determine what deserves attention, what can be ignored, and what must remain hidden indefinitely.

Algorithmic censorship creates a carefully curated mirage of reality. We see what powerful interests decide we should see. Everything else simply vanishes into digital oblivion

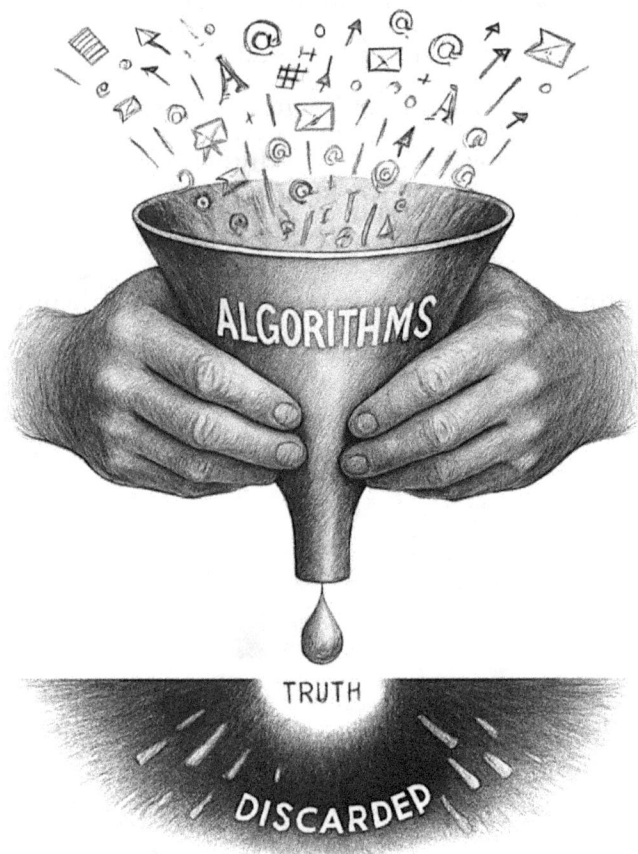

FILTERED REALITY
Algorithmic Truth Bottleneck

Digital Truth-Seeking: Tools for the Modern Investigator

Navigating the digital black vault requires new investigative tools. The modern truth-seeker must become adept at digital forensics, encryption, anonymous browsing, and understanding algorithmic biases. This skill set represents a new literacy for survival in the digital age, as crucial as reading and writing once were.

In this digital landscape, no source can be trusted implicitly. Documents and leaks must be scrutinized for authenticity, motives examined, and corroboration rigorously sought. Understanding the methodologies of digital suppression and how to circumvent them becomes essential to navigating this treacherous terrain.

This chapter, and this book, equips you with those tools—methods for bypassing censorship, decrypting propaganda, and uncovering digital footprints that others prefer you never see.

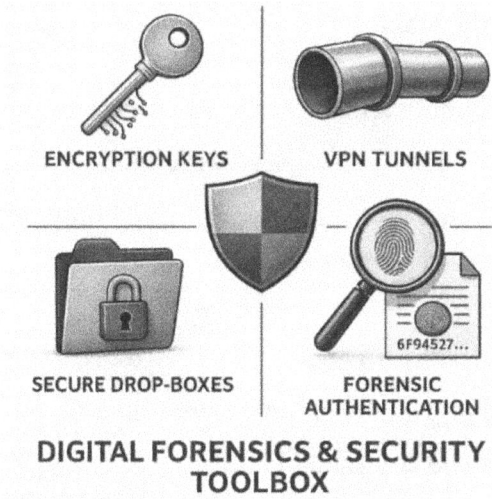

ENCRYPTION KEYS   VPN TUNNELS

SECURE DROP-BOXES   FORENSIC
                       AUTHENTICATION

DIGITAL FORENSICS & SECURITY TOOLBOX

The Responsibility of Knowing

In the age of digital secrecy, knowing how to find and authenticate suppressed information is your most powerful weapon.

Gaining access to forbidden information is exhilarating, but it comes with a profound responsibility. Truth can liberate, but mishandled, it can also inflame, confuse, or provoke harmful consequences. Ethical disclosure is as crucial as truth discovery.

The digital black vault isn't just about suppressed data—it's about the profound impact that revelation can have on societies, governments, and individual lives. The decision to release hidden truths demands careful judgment, integrity, and courage.

Breaking Open the Vault

The digital black vault remains a formidable force, yet its walls are beginning to crack. Every leak, every whistleblower, every exposure is a hammer strike against secrecy. Truth, once glimpsed, can never be unseen.

Now, reader, it is your turn. You possess the tools, you understand the stakes, and you grasp the profound responsibility of revelation. You have glimpsed behind the digital curtain.

Use this knowledge wisely, bravely, and relentlessly. The vault can only remain locked if we choose not to see what lies within.

TRUTH UNBOUND

Part IV: Beyond the Redacted Lines

Chapter 11: The Patterns of Suppression

The greatest threat to the powerful is not revolution, but revelation.

It's no accident that history's most guarded truths remain under lock and key, protected by a maze of redacted texts, secret archives, and the elusive whispers of those who once knew but dared not speak. Yet, even the most careful censor leaves behind patterns—recurring signatures, mechanisms, and psychological motives—that betray a deeper conspiracy: the universal impulse among ruling powers to control knowledge. Understanding these patterns is not just an academic exercise; it is a matter of reclaiming humanity's right to a truthful past and, perhaps, to a more honest future.

In this chapter, we embark upon an investigative journey, mapping the intricate choreography of concealment practiced across millennia. We will illuminate how, despite vast temporal and geographic divides, the tactics of suppression echo consistently. Through this lens, seemingly disconnected acts of censorship—from ancient Alexandria to modern digital blackouts—emerge as pieces of a singular puzzle: the preservation of power at the expense of truth.

What These Cases Reveal in Common

The cases examined throughout this book—ancient forbidden artifacts, buried government experiments, lost manuscripts, and suspicious archaeological silences—share one profound similarity: all contain information perceived as dangerous to established authority. The question of why certain truths are dangerous is central to our understanding.

In nearly every instance, whether it's the erasure of prehistoric civilizations discovered by archaeologists or the active destruction of early scientific writings that contradicted religious dogma, the act of suppression arises precisely at the point where new knowledge challenges entrenched belief systems or threatens political dominance. This pattern has a distinctly predictable character:

- **First**, evidence is discovered, often unexpectedly, contradicting prevailing doctrines.
- **Second**, authoritative bodies react defensively, labelling such evidence as false, heretical, or conspiratorial.
- **Third**, the original discoverers or proponents are discredited— sometimes violently, always methodically.
- **Lastly**, the evidence itself vanishes, quietly relegated to what we term the "dark archives."

The Psychology of Control: Why Truth is Dangerous

Truth challenges narratives. Narratives legitimize power. Thus, truths that disrupt accepted narratives are inherently destabilizing. From

The Four Stages of Suppression:

1. *Discovery of Threatening Information*
2. *Institutional Denial and Defamation*
3. *Removal or Silencing of Sources*
4. *Erasure from Historical Memory*

religious institutions like the medieval Church, which waged war against heretical astronomy, to authoritarian regimes intent on rewriting their past, controlling the truth is about maintaining psychological dominance over populations.

Truth introduces uncertainty, and uncertainty breeds dissent. Dissent inspires action, and action threatens established order. The powerful intuitively understand this progression and respond by closing ranks around "acceptable" knowledge. Suppressed truths frequently uncover weaknesses or injustices within a power structure, potentially provoking unrest, rebellion, or revolution. For authority, suppression is not just practical—it is instinctual.

Human psychology itself is a crucial factor. Social psychologists have documented how cognitive dissonance—the discomfort we feel when confronted with conflicting beliefs—can cause entire societies to reject well-supported evidence. Suppressors exploit this psychology, knowing that people prefer comfortable illusions over troubling facts.

Why Powerful Institutions Fear Truth:

- *Truth undermines established legitimacy.*
- *Truth exposes vulnerabilities within power structures.*
- *Truth incites psychological discomfort, fostering*

Mapping the "Chain of Silence" Across Centuries

While forms of suppression have evolved, the underlying tactics remain remarkably stable, forming a "chain of silence" linking ancient rulers to modern governments. Consider:

- The burning of the Great Library of Alexandria: valuable knowledge that contradicted dominant political or religious ideologies was systematically erased.

- Medieval inquisitions: control was exerted through widespread persecution, fear, and elimination of dissenting texts.

- Modern classified archives: states claim national security justifications, yet frequently the withheld information pertains more to covering embarrassments than to actual security threats.

Despite technological advancements, the fundamentals of suppression remain: control access, control interpretation, control memory.

Today's digital realm provides a particularly stark illustration. Algorithms selectively present or bury information, quietly shaping collective memory. Entire events, reports, or controversies vanish overnight, lost beneath an ever-expanding digital heap. The "chain of silence," once literal, has become metaphorical yet no less binding.

CYCLE OF SILENCE
THE EVOLUTION OF SUPPRESSION

Ancient	Medieval	Modern

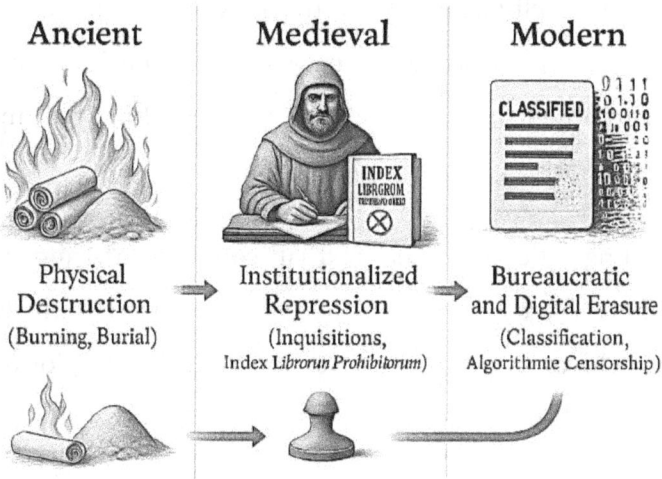

Physical Destruction	Institutionalized Repression	Bureaucratic and Digital Erasure
(Burning, Burial)	(Inquisitions, Index *Librorun Prohibitorum*)	(Classification, Algorithmie Censorship)

Inspired by timelines from *HistoryOfInformation.com* and
American Libraries Magazine

The Evolution of Suppression:

- *Ancient: Physical Destruction (Burning, Burial)*
- *Medieval: Institutionalized Repression (Inquisitions, Index Librorum Prohibitorum)*
- *Modern: Bureaucratic and Digital Erasure (Classification, Algorithmic Censorship)*

Unmasking the Patterns: Tools of the Investigator

Recognizing suppression's fingerprints requires investigators to understand the tell-tale marks authorities leave behind. Redacted documents bear linguistic and visual clues: inconsistent censoring, references to absent materials, abrupt narrative shifts—all indicating removed sections.

Likewise, linguistic forensics, textual comparisons, and metadata analysis have become crucial. Researchers now routinely cross-reference archives across multiple jurisdictions, looking for omissions or contradictions.

Investigative Toolkit:

- *Linguistic Forensics (Detecting edits and redactions)*
- *Cross-Referencing (Identifying narrative inconsistencies across sources)*
- *Metadata Analysis (Uncovering digital footprints indicating suppression)*

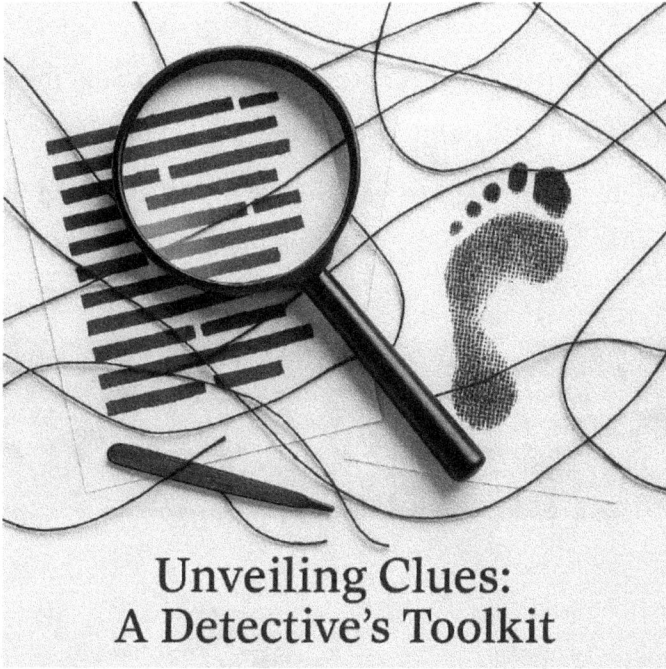

Unveiling Clues:
A Detective's Toolkit

We inhabit an era where suppression grows increasingly sophisticated, cloaked in digital invisibility and administrative obscurity. The price of ignorance is steep; history forgotten is history repeated. Vigilance, skepticism, and curiosity form the triumvirate of resistance against the perpetual chain of silence.

As readers—now investigators yourselves—you are empowered to challenge what's presented as unquestionable. History, as it turns out, is far more fluid and contested than textbooks admit. The redacted lines invite your scrutiny; the hidden files await your discernment.

Illuminating the Dark Archives

Suppression thrives in silence; transparency is its antidote. This exploration into patterns of suppression reveals not only the universal tactics of powerful entities but also the universal obligation to question, challenge, and illuminate. The dark archives, no matter how deep their recesses, cannot extinguish the enduring human drive toward truth.

> *Suppression may obscure truth, but it cannot erase it. Truth, like water, inevitably seeps through the smallest cracks.*

Chapter 12

Reconstructing the Lost Record

Within the shadowed corridors of history, where official narratives falter and documentation fades into deliberate obscurity, lies an irresistible call to those with the courage to question. When the ink on historical documents blots over crucial evidence and key facts vanish mysteriously between archived volumes, we find ourselves standing before a locked door—a door guarding not just secrets, but power itself.

This book has guided you through the labyrinth of suppressed truths, but now comes the most critical juncture: reconstructing the lost record. How can ordinary individuals sift through layers of misinformation and deliberate obfuscation to reveal a more truthful past? This chapter equips you with the critical thinking and research methodologies you need.

Let's begin your transformation from passive receiver to active researcher of the forbidden truth.

How to Think Critically about Official Narratives

Official narratives shape our world. They determine what we remember, how we interpret events, and even how we define ourselves. Yet, to accept official history without scrutiny is to surrender our intellect to powers whose interests rarely align with truth.

Consider three critical steps to challenge any official narrative:

1. Question the Origin

Official histories often emerge from power centers—governments, religious authorities, and elite academic institutions. Investigate the source: What was their vested interest? Was it political control, ideological conformity, or societal stability?

2. Identify the Gaps

Historical narratives rarely tell the whole story. Watch for unexplained leaps, suppressed controversies, and notable absences. Gaps in the record are not simply accidents but deliberate silences, signals of what may be hidden.

THE MYTH OF OBJECTIVITY

Remember, no narrative is neutral. Every story has a teller with motives, biases, and blind spots. Always ask yourself: Who benefits from this particular telling?

THE CENSORED CODEX

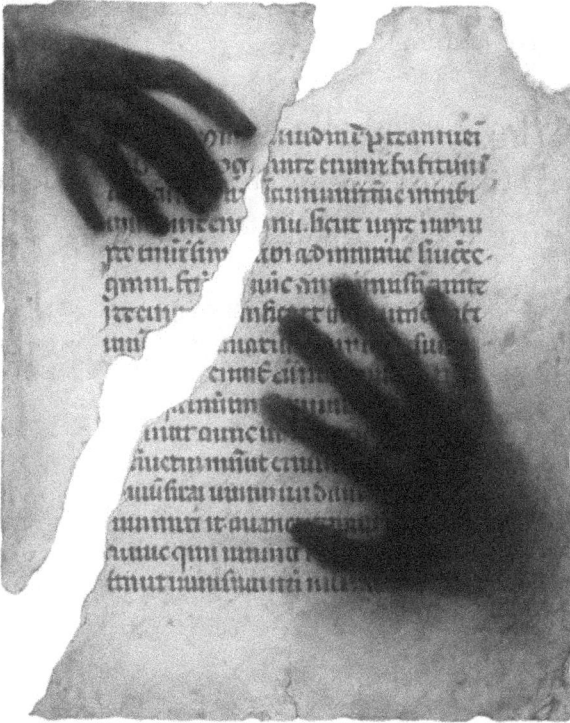

3. Trace Alternative Voices

Official history marginalizes voices that threaten its coherence. Seek out these marginal perspectives—letters, diaries, censored books, and oral traditions—because truth often survives on the periphery.

Tools for Independent Research and Connecting the Dots

Historical suppression thrives on fragmentation. Power relies on the compartmentalization of knowledge to keep people from seeing larger patterns. But with deliberate strategies and accessible tools, anyone can reconstruct suppressed histories.

Tool #1: Archive Mining

Despite secrecy, most archives contain overlooked documents waiting for rediscovery. Classified papers, once released under Freedom of Information laws, can rewrite history.

THE THREE CORE TOOLS FOR INDEPENDENT RESEARCH

- *Archive Mining: Learning to navigate public archives, special collections, and digital repositories.*
- *Open Source Intelligence (OSINT): Leveraging publicly available data to uncover hidden connections.*
- *Narrative Mapping: Visualizing timelines, events, and individuals to spot hidden links and patterns.*

Tool #2: Open Source Intelligence (OSINT)

OSINT techniques evolved in intelligence circles but are now available to citizens. Search engines, metadata analysis, and social media forensics allow you to reconstruct hidden histories piece by piece.

Tool #3: Narrative Mapping

A CITIZEN'S CHECKLIST FOR OSINT

- *Who authored this source, and why?*
- *Can claims be cross-referenced independently?*
- *What patterns emerge when you place this information in a broader context?*

Connecting historical dots requires visual aids. Creating timelines or interactive maps can transform disjointed facts into coherent narratives. Software exists to help visualize data in ways once exclusive to intelligence analysts.

Case File: Citizen Researchers Who Rewrote History

History is not solely shaped by trained historians or government archivists. Often, ordinary individuals driven by curiosity or injustice have forced monumental revisions of the historical record.

The Footprints That Shattered Timelines

When Mary Leakey uncovered footprints in Tanzania, dated at nearly 3.6 million years, academia balked at their implications. The established narrative—that modern humans emerged much later—was threatened by this discovery.

The Suppressed Antiquity of Humanity

Citizen researcher Michael Cremo exemplifies reconstructing suppressed history. His work, meticulously investigating forgotten 19th-century anthropological reports, revealed extensive evidence of

Truth is uncomfortable to institutions, particularly when it demands revisions to textbooks and established authority.

human antiquity millions of years older than officially recognized. Institutions ignored findings that conflicted with Darwinian timelines, yet these records existed, waiting for rediscovery.

Cremo's findings shook established archeology by confronting academia with credible evidence of humanity's deeper past—evidence long discarded to maintain scholarly orthodoxy.

Rediscovering the Forbidden Sites

From secret Nazi sanctuaries like Himmler's Wewelsburg Castle, where grotesque rituals attempted to rewrite spiritual history, to private banking houses guarding monarchic treasures, the most powerful revelations were often sparked by private citizens or independent journalists shining light on hidden sanctuaries.

Reclaiming Your Power as a Historical Investigator

Today's digital age offers unprecedented opportunities to reclaim historical agency from institutions. With open-source platforms and digital archives, history has never been so available—or vulnerable-to—to reinterpretation by independent researchers.

Consider these empowering steps:

1. **Identify and preserve digital evidence**: Always download, archive, and screenshot digital documents that might disappear.

2. **Triangulate your sources:** Cross-reference everything—official documents, eyewitness accounts, leaked materials.

3. **Create collaborative networks:** Share findings and insights within communities of fellow researchers. History is reclaimed most powerfully when people collaborate.

The Ethical Responsibility of Unveiling Truth

Uncovering hidden histories carries ethical implications. Truths buried beneath official records often expose uncomfortable realities. It is crucial to handle revelations with care and responsibility, providing context rather than sensationalism, and clarity rather than chaos.

The Transformative Power of Questioning History

Reconstructing suppressed histories is not merely an academic exercise. It fundamentally alters perceptions, disrupts power dynamics, and empowers marginalized voices.

Every revealed truth chips away at societal complacency. Each act of historical reclamation moves humanity closer to understanding its authentic past, liberating us from narratives engineered to limit freedom, curiosity, and potential.

You now possess the tools, strategies, and inspiration to become an investigator into histories that the powerful prefer to be hidden. Remember: each hidden record discovered, each suppressed fact reclaimed, is an act of liberation.

Reconstructing history is revolutionary. But the revolution requires commitment, courage, and relentless curiosity.

The lost records are waiting. The pen to rewrite history is now yours.

THE RESEARCHER'S CODE

- *Verify your findings independently.*
- *Present evidence transparently.*
- *Always distinguish between confirmed facts, strong inference, and pure speculation.*

Chapter 13

What Lies Ahead

Why Suppressed History Matters Now More Than Ever

There is a certain kind of blindness woven deeply into the fabric of official history. It is not accidental, nor is it simply due to the chaos of passing centuries. Rather, it is carefully orchestrated by those whose power is sustained by maintaining a controlled narrative. The omission or redaction of certain truths serves as a stabilizing force for institutions and societies, creating a version of history designed to sustain the current hierarchies of influence. Yet, as humanity hurtles deeper into the twenty-first century—an era dominated by digital media, artificial intelligence, algorithmic control, and information wars—the cost of such intentional blindness has become painfully clear.

Consider for a moment how the internet has transformed the battleground over historical truths. Today, a single leaked document or photograph can ignite a global political firestorm. Equally potent is the power of suppression, as algorithms and content moderators invisibly decide which information reaches the public eye and which sinks silently into oblivion. This modern form of censorship may

> When history is hidden or censored, societies lose the wisdom of past mistakes, becoming vulnerable to repeating catastrophic failures. Knowledge is not just power—it is survival.

appear subtle, yet its effects are profound. It shapes our perceptions, guiding our collective memory toward approved versions of the past and away from troubling, inconvenient truths.

Historical censorship matters today more than ever because we stand on the precipice of unprecedented technological control over our shared consciousness. If history continues to be shaped only by gatekeepers—be they government censors, academic elites, or corporate interests—we face a future stripped of critical insight, reduced to a landscape of managed realities.

The Future of Disclosure, Archives, and Citizen Truth-Seekers

We now live in the paradoxical age of transparency and secrecy. While powerful entities tighten their grasp on historical narratives, the tools of disclosure have never been more accessible to ordinary individuals. The barriers between classified truths and the public domain have become more porous, thanks to digital technology, whistleblower platforms, and the democratization of information.

Yet the future of disclosure is uncertain. We face two possible trajectories:

First, a bleak landscape dominated by digital authoritarianism, where dissenting voices and uncomfortable truths are algorithmically silenced, classified behind endless digital firewalls. In this scenario, truth-seekers risk marginalization or worse, criminalization.

Second, a brighter scenario in which citizen truth-seekers gain unprecedented power, aided by digital archives, blockchain-protected evidence, decentralized internet platforms, and open-source intelligence (OSINT) methodologies. In this future, hidden truths will not remain hidden for long, and suppressed histories will resurface, recalibrating humanity's understanding of itself.

The choice between these futures rests largely in the hands of today's truth-seekers. The tools of disclosure—crowdsourced archives, encrypted whistleblower channels, digital forensics, and metadata analysis—are no longer restricted to intelligence operatives or investigative journalists alone. These tools belong now to anyone willing to engage seriously with evidence.

Citizen Truth-Seekers: Guardians of Future History

The digital revolution has democratized investigative power, turning ordinary citizens into frontline defenders of historical integrity.

> *Every smartphone can become a weapon against historical censorship, every citizen a potential archivist in the battle for truth.*

Already, individuals worldwide are piecing together hidden narratives from leaked emails, FOIA requests, archival research, and sophisticated analytical tools. The success of platforms like WikiLeaks, independent journalism collectives, and open-source research networks proves the unstoppable potential of collaborative truth-seeking.

Future citizen archivists and truth-seekers will build upon current methodologies, creating expansive databases of suppressed knowledge accessible to all. They will employ advanced algorithms not for censorship, but for the precise opposite: exposing inconsistencies, anomalies, and cover-ups across vast swathes of digital data. AI-driven metadata analysis and global blockchain repositories will ensure records remain unalterable and immune to censorship, becoming permanent reminders of historical truth.

A Call to Uncover Your Hidden Truths

As you conclude this investigative journey through suppressed history, you stand at a unique crossroads. You now possess the keys—tools, insights, and methodologies—to unlock hidden archives and question sanitized narratives. But beyond merely absorbing knowledge, you have a deeper responsibility: to apply these principles actively in your pursuit of truth.

This book has laid the groundwork, but the true power of disclosure lies in your hands. Begin your investigations:

- **Start Locally:** Unearth suppressed local histories within your community. The records may be closer—and far more significant—than you realize.

- **Question Authority:** Apply critical analysis to accepted narratives. Examine the motives behind historical omissions or alterations.

- **Contribute Globally:** Share your discoveries through open-source platforms. Join networks of digital historians and citizen journalists to amplify your voice and findings.

In every suppressed truth lies the seed of transformative potential. By reclaiming hidden narratives, you can reshape society's collective understanding, bringing to light the injustices and manipulations embedded within official histories. Your commitment to uncovering hidden truths will ripple across time, altering future narratives and empowering generations yet unborn.

The Responsibility of Knowledge

Yet with great insight comes significant responsibility. Truth-seeking must be guided by integrity, discernment, and rigorous verification. The same technologies used to uncover suppressed history can also propagate misinformation, confusion, and harmful conspiracies. Vigilance against these pitfalls is essential.

Suppressed history is not just about conspiracies—it is about power, justice, and the right to an informed reality. You hold the power to reclaim that reality.

Approach each new revelation with caution but courage. Remain open to evidence but critical of claims lacking substantiation. Your goal is not merely exposure, but clarification. Genuine truth-seekers aim to illuminate rather than sensationalize.

Truth without discernment leads to confusion; discernment without truth leads to cynicism. Balance is the cornerstone of authentic discovery.

BEACON OF CLARITY

The Legacy You Leave

In choosing to engage actively with suppressed history, you become more than just a reader—you become a participant in the ongoing struggle over memory and truth. Each recovered document, each verified fact, each historical correction represents a victory over institutional silence and manipulation.

Imagine a world where future historians look back and find a trove of evidence preserved not by official institutions but by ordinary people like yourself, committed citizens who refused to let critical truths disappear. This is the profound legacy you can leave.

The archives have been opened, the tools are in your grasp, and the choice is yours. Will you accept this invitation, joining countless others dedicated to preserving the integrity of human history? The future of truth itself depends upon your answer.

Beyond the Redacted Lines

As we close the pages of this book, remember this fundamental truth: real power fears knowledge. That is precisely why some truths are so meticulously buried. Yet, despite the formidable forces of suppression, history repeatedly proves resilient, surfacing through cracks in censorship to rewrite our collective memory.

In stepping beyond the redacted lines, you have glimpsed a world more complex, unsettling, yet infinitely richer than conventional narratives suggest. Embrace that complexity. Pursue that discomfort. Your courage in questioning, in seeking, in revealing the hidden will echo through generations.

You have been given the map. Now, chart your course through the archives still waiting to be opened. What lies ahead is a world no longer defined by ignorance and suppression, but illuminated by the courage of citizens determined to reclaim their history.

History belongs not to those who hide it, but to those brave enough to rediscover it.

Bonus Section: Dark Archives Workbook

Companion guide to **Dark Archives — Suppressed Stories, Secret Documents, and the Conspiracies Buried Beneath Official History.**

How to use this workbook

This volume turns the big ideas in **Dark Archives** into an eight-module learning journey. Each module contains:

1. **Briefing** – distilled theory from the book (with page references).

2. **Exercises & labs** – step-by-step activities that sharpen archival-sleuthing skills.

3. **Critical-thinking drills** – checklists that stress-test claims.

4. **Journal prompts** – space to interrogate your own "official truths."

5. **Action project** – a mini-investigation you can complete with open-source tools.

Work at your own pace or form a reading circle; every module ends with a peer-review rubric so groups can trade feedback.

Module 1 · Opening the Vault

Learning goals
• Define a *dark archive* in its three forms (literal secrecy, cultural amnesia, digital obfuscation).   • Recognise the "knowledge filter."

Briefing

Power's first instinct is not to invent new lies but to hide old truths. That hiding creates blind spots large enough to bend civilisation's timeline — and your own perception of reality.

Exercise 1.1 – Map your personal filter

List five moments from local or family history you know only through a single source. For each, identify what *might* be missing (voices? documents?). Spend 15 minutes free-writing on how that gap could tilt your understanding.

_____

_____

_____

_____

_____

_____

_____

_____

_____

_____

_____

_____

Critical-thinking drill: The Three-Question Test

1. Who benefits from this narrative?

_____

2. What evidence can be independently verified?

_____
_____
_____
_____
_____
_____

3. Where are the gaps, and why do they persist?

_____
_____
_____
_____
_____
_____
_____

You can also copy the above three questions onto an index card and tape it beside your screen. Use it every time a "fact" scrolls past your feed.

Journal prompt

Which official story about your community have you never doubted—and why?

_____

_____

_____

_____

_____

_____

_____

_____

_____

_____

Module 2 · Suppressed Evidence

Learning goals
<ul><li>Describe "knowledge filtration" in archaeology.</li><li>Evaluate three case studies (Table Mountain, Klerksdorp spheres, Piri Reis map).</li></ul>

Briefing

From obsidian spear-points found *under* 33-million-year-old basalt at Table Mountain to grooved metallic orbs dated 2.8 billion years, anomalies follow a four-stage eclipse: **Discovery** → **Ridicule** → **Misplacement** → **Silence**.

Exercise 2.1 – Stratigraphy on a shoestring

Using free GIS layers for your region, plot one location where Pleistocene gravels lie under volcanic caprock. Hypothesize what artefacts, if found there, would threaten current models.

_____

_____

_____

_____

_____

_____

_____

_____

_____

_____

_____

_____

_____

Lab 2.2 – CT-scan thought experiment

Sketch a protocol for testing a coal-embedded artefact with non-destructive CT imaging. What chain-of-custody steps guarantee authenticity? Reference the "Toolkit for the Modern Heretic."

Action project

Draft a two-page mini-FOIA request template seeking shipping or accession records for a single "lost" Table Mountain artefact. Submit (or simulate) and record response times.

_____

_____

_____

Module 3 · Conspiracies in Plain Sight

Learning goals

- Reconstruct the life-cycle of MK-Ultra, Operation Northwoods & Blue Book.

- Spot the four-step state-suppression recipe: Delay – Dilute – Defame – Delegate.

Briefing

No programme shows the government's war on truth better than MK-Ultra: 80+ universities, hidden grants, files shredded on exit.

Exercise 3.1 – Primary-source autopsy

Declassifications arrive bathed in ink. Download one MK-Ultra sub-project PDF, highlight every redaction block, and categorise (identity, method, location). How does each blank skew the interpretation?

_____

_____

_____

_____

_____

_____

_____

_____

_____

_____

_____

_____

_____

_____

_____

_____

_____

_____

_____

_____

Critical-thinking checklist: Is it disinformation?

1. *Timestamp mismatch* – do key events surface only after a purge? Explain.

_____

_____

_____

2. *Authoritative thinness* – does rebuttal rely on rank, not data? Explain.

_____

_____

_____

3. *Echo amplitude* – are dismissals repeated verbatim across outlets? Explain.

_____

_____

_____

4. *Sanction asymmetry* – are whistle-blowers punished more than perpetrators? Explain.

_____

_____

_____

Validate each flag with an example from MK-Ultra or Northwoods.

Journal prompt

Recall a moment you first heard a "conspiracy theory" later proved true. How did confirmation change your trust threshold?

_____

_____

_____

_____

_____

_____

_____

_____

Module 4 · The Machinery of Secrecy

Learning goals
• Identify institutional motives (state security, doctrine, profit).   • Apply budget-sleuthing to spot black projects.

Briefing

Delay is the most elegant censor: a 75-year seal outlives witnesses and defuses outrage — hence the archivists' term **deep freeze**.

Exercise 4.1 – Budget autopsy

Collect three consecutive defence-appropriations bills. Track any line-item with sudden ≥ 20 % growth yet vague wording ("Advanced Aerospace Threats"). Draft a one-paragraph hypothesis of the hidden operation.

_____

_____

_____

_____

_____

_____

_____

Peer-review rubric

Criterion	0	1	2	3
Uses at least two independent budget sources				
Links growth to geopolitical events				
Suggests verification pathway (FOIA, satellite)				

Score 3 = publishable mini-dossier.

Module 5 · Tools of the Twenty-First-Century Truth-Seeker

Learning goals
• Practice FOIA sequencing, metadata hunting, and triangulation. • Build a personal digital forensics kit.

Checklist: Your basic kit

- FOIA bot account
- Offline metadata-scraper

- EXIF scrubber & validator
- Zero-knowledge cloud vault

Log each tool's install date and last update; stale tools are broken tools.

Lab 5.1 – Metadata bingo

Download any "sanitised" PDF from an official site. Run it through your scraper. Note creation time, last modification, and software version. Does the timeline align with the document's cover date?

_____

_____

_____

_____

_____

_____

_____

Module 6 · Economics of Silence

Learning goals
• Explain how capital throttles research (grant bias, patent seizure).

Briefing

Free energy threatens commodity markets; the simplest burial method is a quiet *buy-out + NDA + export-control lock*. See "The Suppression Toolkit".

Exercise 6.1 – Patent grave-digging

Search the USPTO for "water-fuel cell" patents that lapsed after assignment to defence contractors. Chart status changes on a timeline. Does lapse coincide with classified funding spikes?

_____

_____

_____

_____

_____

_____

_____

Module 7 · Cognitive Debiasing

Guided reflection

Write two pages on a topic where you are *certain* the mainstream is wrong. Identify evidence tiers (anecdote, document, triangulated fact). Mark your weakest link. Revise belief strength accordingly.

Group activity

Hold a "Devil's Advocate" debate. Defenders present an anomaly (e.g., Klerksdorp spheres). Skeptics apply the three-tier filter (Ridicule/Reinterpret/Remove). Rotate roles.

Do well to share your findings below...

_____

_____

_____

_____

_____

_____

Module 8 · Capstone Investigation

Choose one archive, collection, or sealed case from **Dark Archives**.
Over four weeks:

1. **Scoping** – craft a precise research question.
2. **Acquisition** – file at least one information request or scrape an open dataset.
3. **Analysis** – triangulate with two secondary sources.
4. **Publication** – produce a 1500-word brief or 10-slide deck.

Answer the four questions in the space created below...

The rubric mirrors the peer-review grid from Module 4. Your mentor or group signs off.

_____

_____

_____

_____

_____

_____

_____

_____

_____

_____

_____

_____

_____

_____

_____

_____

_____

_____

_____

_____

_____

_____

_____

_____

_____

Bonus Section

A. Timeline of Major Suppressed Discoveries

Year (discovered/declassified)	Event
1849-1890	*Table Mountain* obsidian artefacts found beneath Miocene basalt; boxed and forgotten
1929 / 1960s	**Piri Reis map** examined; hints at ice-free Antarctic coast centuries before discovery.
1953-1973 / 2001	**MK-Ultra** runs, shredded, then partially released.
1962 / 1997	**Operation Northwoods** proposal revealed
1967-1980 / ongoing	Nuclear-correlated UAP incidents logged, still partly classified.
1994 / 2000s	**Göbekli Tepe** upends civilisation chronology.

(Expand this table as you encounter new cases.)

B. Critical-Thinking Checklist for Spotting Disinformation

1. **Provenance gap** – Who first reported the claim?

2. **Compression ratio** – Are complex facts reduced to slogans?

3. **Echo uniformity** – Identical phrasing across outlets?

4. **Stakeholder silence** – Experts in the field studiously ignore it?

5. **Ad hominem tell** – Critics attack the messenger, not the evidence.

Use with *The Three-Question Test* (Module 1).

C. Guided Journal Prompts

1. Which three *official* historical events feel least plausible to you, and what evidence *would* change your mind?

_____

_____

_____

_____

_____

_____

_____

_____

_____

_____

2. Recall a family story that clashes with textbook history. Draft interview questions for the oldest living relative.

_____

_____

_____

_____

_____

_____

_____

_____

_____

_____

_____

_____

3. "History is written by the victors—but edited by the powerful". Write 300 words on how that sentence reframes an event you studied in school.

D. Resource Library

Archive / Tool	What It Holds	Access Tip
CIA CREST	13M pages of declassified ops incl. MK-Ultra fragments	Use advanced search filters; sort by release date
National Archives – UK	Signals-intelligence files (ECHELON, UAP)	FOI requests lapse after 30 years; cite "public interest" override
The Black Vault	3,000+ FOIA'd U.S. defence docs	Cross-check PDFs for hidden layers / OCR text
Vatican Apostolic Archives	53 miles of shelving; medieval to WWII dossiers	Entry requires an academic sponsor; apply a year ahead
Open Corporates	225 M corporate records	Trace shell companies funding "black projects"
Bellingcat Toolkit	OSINT guides & forum	Follow their metadata and geolocation tutorials

(Append your local resources as you progress.)

Truth does not fear the light; only power does. May this workbook light your path through archives—paper, digital, or whispered—and sharpen the courage required to keep them open.

Conclusion

Official history, as this investigation has shown, is less a neutral chronicle than a carefully managed script—pages excised, margins blacked, timelines massaged to protect the hierarchies of state, creed, academy, and capital. Each chapter has peeled back a layer of that script: Miocene spear-points boxed into oblivion, mind-control files shredded on command, energy patents entombed in export-control vaults, and propaganda loops that fossilise into "accepted" memory. Taken together, these cases reveal a single pattern: **power's first reflex is not to invent lies but to hide truths.**

Yet the very era that refines censorship also furnishes its antidote. Encrypted drop-boxes, blockchain timestamps, and open-source intelligence turn every whistle-blower's laptop into a portable archive, every citizen into a potential curator of the historical record. In this paradoxical age of transparency-and-secrecy, the barriers between classified vault and public domain have never been thinner—or more fiercely defended.

The task ahead, therefore, splits into two:

1. **Relentless Excavation** – Continue prying at the knowledge filter wherever it appears: in budget line-items suddenly swelling by 20 percent, in peer-review gatekeeping, in algorithmic burials that push inconvenient search results beyond the first page. Your toolkit now includes FOIA sequencers, metadata forensics, and triangulation grids that can spotlight silence as clearly as speech.

2. **Ethical Stewardship** – Truth without discernment breeds chaos; discernment without truth breeds cynicism. Apply both. Verify hashes, weigh provenance, and remember that leaked data can harm as easily as it can heal. **Illumination is not the same as sensationalism.**

Why does this matter now? Because digital authoritarianism can algorithmically erase yesterday's leak before lunch, and because societies stripped of contested memory stumble into catastrophes they no longer recognise. Conversely, a single declassified page—properly contextualised—can unseat dictators, rewrite textbooks, or spark technologies once deemed impossible.

The final choice sits with you. Will the discoveries on these pages harden into mere curiosities, or will they galvanise a new cadre of **citizen archivists** who treat every smartphone as a weapon against historical amnesia?

Truth does not fear the light; only power does. Stand in that light. Widen the crack in the vault. And may future historians find, in your courage, the proof that archives—no matter how dark—can never stay closed forever.

www.ingramcontent.com/pod-product-compliance
Lightning Source LLC
Chambersburg PA
CBHW050119280326
41933CB00010B/1161